Praise for *The Good of Giving Up*

For many modern Christians, Lent is a strange ritual that "other" people do. This should not be! Christians have observed a period of Easter preparation from the very beginning of church history. For those who are interested in Lent but don't know where to begin, Aaron Damiani's book is the perfect introduction. With biblical expertise and a pastor's heart, Damiani invites modern Christians who are skeptical of Lent into its true meaning: deeper union with Jesus Himself. Don't miss out on what Lent has to offer. Let this wise Anglican pastor lead you into the spiritual riches of the risen Christ.

BRYAN LITFIN
Professor of Historical Theology, Moody Bible Institute, and author of *After Acts*

This book will help Christians who are just discovering the practice of observing Lent or who need fresh inspiration regarding how to make their observation more meaningful. It is insightful, practical, and grounded in a wise understanding of our historic Christian faith. It will encourage you to discover how good giving up can be!

RUTH HALEY BARTON
Founder, Transforming Center, and author of *Sacred Rhythms and Life Together in Christ*

Aaron has done the church a great service by taking Lent, something many think is only for the "those other churches" or the super spiritual, and showing us why it is important for every follower of Jesus. His clear explanations and practical tips remove the confusion from this topic and make it possible for everyone to understand and practice Lent. I can't wait to recommend Aaron's book to our church!

JACKSON CRUM
Lead Pastor, Park Community Church, Chicago

Our deepest hunger is for bread that only Christ can provide. Anyone who knows this cherishes practices that reorder our desires and direct our longing toward Christ. Aaron has given us a clear and compelling way of entering into Lent as a life-giving spiritual practice. Pastoral, conversational, and practical, this book is a marvelous invitation to journey with Jesus through death and resurrection.

GLENN PACKIAM
Lead Pastor, New Life Downtown, a co
Colorado Springs, and author of *Discov*

In his preaching, pastoring, and personal life, Aaron Damiani is a gift to the church. A remarkable primer on the most overlooked season of the Christian year, *The Good of Giving Up* grounds and connects Christians of every background to our perennial need for God's gifts in the wilderness. I am grateful for this passionate introduction to Lent, at once challenging and inspirational. I will embrace the Lenten season more deeply because of this book.

PAUL J. PASTOR
Author of *The Face of the Deep*

Lent, like any unfamiliar practice, is best explored with a competent guide. *The Good of Giving Up* is just that. Aaron beautifully sets forth the practices of Lent as a gentle harness, yoking us to the goodness and power of Christ. Get in a Lenten yoke with Jesus and you'll discover that is not heavy or ill-fitting, but food for the soul.

TODD HUNTER
Founding pastor of Holy Trinity Anglican Church in Costa Mesa, CA, and author of *Our Favorite Sins*

For too long, Christianity has been dancing without any rhythm or beat. But to dance, we need music. Therein lies the brilliance of what Damiani does here. In these pages, we hear the music of Lent, if we are willing. This book invites us to a whole new rhythm that is both ancient and fresh.

A. J. SWOBODA
Pastor of Theophilus in Portland, OR, and author of *The Dusty Ones*

In a historical moment when the church seeks to stand on her toes to apprehend the inestimable beauty, excellence, and glorious light of Christ, Aaron makes a counterintuitive case: these gifts are not realized by self-elevation or white-knuckled effort; they come by following the sacrificial trajectory of the incarnate Son. Toward this end, he focuses on the manifold opportunities afforded by the Lenten season, making a case for its importance and forging a path toward its realization.

CHRIS CASTALDO
Lead Pastor of New Covenant Church in Naperville, IL, and author of *Talking with Catholics about the Gospel*

THE
GOOD
OF
GIVING
UP

Discovering the Freedom of Lent

A A R O N   D A M I A N I

MOODY PUBLISHERS

CHICAGO

© 2017 by
AARON DAMIANI

Names and details of some stories have been changed to protect the privacy of individuals.

Edited by Kevin P. Emmert
Interior and cover design: Erik M. Peterson
Cover image of hands copyright © 2016 by Pearl / Lightstock (219806)
Author photo: Jill Fager Photography

Library of Congress Cataloging-in-Publication Data

Names: Damiani, Aaron, author.
Title: The good of giving up : discovering the freedom of Lent / Aaron
    Damiani.
Description: Chicago : Moody Publishers, [2017] | Includes bibliographical
    references.
Identifiers: LCCN 2016043806 (print) | LCCN 2016046427 (ebook) | ISBN
    9780802415165 | ISBN 9780802495242
Subjects: LCSH: Lent.
Classification: LCC BV85 .D29 2017 (print) | LCC BV85 (ebook) | DDC
    263/.92--dc23
LC record available at https://lccn.loc.gov/2016043806

ISBN: 978-0-8024-1516-5

All websites listed herein are accurate at the time of publication but may change in the future or cease to exist. The listing of website references and resources does not imply publisher endorsement of the site's entire contents. Groups and organizations are listed for informational purposes, and listing does not imply publisher endorsement of their activities.

We hope you enjoy this book from Moody Publishers. Our goal is to provide high-quality, thought-provoking books and products that connect truth to your real needs and challenges. For more information on other books and products written and produced from a biblical perspective, go to www.moodypublishers.com or write to:

Moody Publishers
820 N. LaSalle Boulevard
Chicago, IL 60610

3 5 7 9 10 8 6 4 2

Printed in the United States of America

To Laura, the love of my life and fellow pilgrim on the way;
Thank you for sowing, weeping, and rejoicing with me.
Though your birthday is always in Lent,
Our future is always a Feast,

And I can see Home from our window.

Contents

Acknowledgments

This book is like a quilt, woven together with contributions from a number of beloved friends, congregants, and colleagues. Their creativity and support made writing a book on Lent a joyful process. I am deeply grateful to Drew Dyck and Moody Publishers for believing in me and in this book. Drew, thanks for championing the project, providing expertise, offering guidance on the manuscript, and answering my many questions. Your kindness is simply Canadian. Kevin Emmert, your editorial work and theological input added tremendous value, making each chapter more clear, precise, and readable.

Thank you to the leaders and congregation of Immanuel Anglican Church for making space for me to write this book. At the heart of every vibrant church plant are the loving sacrifices of the saints. I saw your sacrifice three years ago when we launched our church and again this past summer as I stepped back from my normal responsibilities in order to devote full attention to writing. Mad props go to the amazing and dedicated staff team for keeping the ministries of our church thriving, and for letting me interrupt them with random ideas about Lent in the process: Daniel Fager, Nichole Sangha, Susan Raedeke, Mandi Beck, and Jennifer Wood. Ashley Smith provided solid, clear research on the history of Lent that helped me connect the dots. Natalie Nyquist edited many of the chapters early on, making both the prose and the footnotes stronger. Carrie Von Hoff proofread many of the chapters and provided high-level suggestions and line edits. Eva Christensen offered ideas for the use of liturgical and visual arts in Lent. Josh Evans, Aaron Sangha, and David Whited provided theological input and conviviality. The Lenten discipleship group met in the summer and pressed me with insightful questions that shaped the content. Thanks to everyone who heeded my requests for Lent testimonies; your stories kept me grounded in reality. This book is truly an artifact of our church.

Before and during the writing of this book, I drafted off of godly men and women whose positive influence is directly reflected in these pages. Bishop Stewart Ruch modeled the Lenten path early on and showed me how joy and suffering shape the soul on the path of holiness. Bishop, thanks for calling me to follow Jesus with you. Just before I began writing, Bill Gaultiere taught me how to "plow the field" as one yoked to Jesus, going at His pace and in His peace. Bill, your empathy, mentoring, and feedback have been a strong ballast to me. Dan Claire apprenticed me in leading and preaching during Lent and Holy Week when I was wet behind the ears in ministry. Dan, in addition to being a "brother of jackals" (Job 30:29), you are also a model of Lenten generosity. Stephen and Barbara Gauthier have taught me about the church fathers and the history of Lent. Stephen, thank you for your spiritual care and for helping me carry the preaching load at Immanuel this summer. Karen Miller, I am grateful for your tough-love leadership coaching that taught me "Boundaries 3.0" and kept me on target to finish the book on time. Bryan Litfin, I am in your debt for your historical research, your discerning eye, and your encouragement to write this book to the glory of God.

Joshua Rogers, thanks for helping me see reality from the perspective of a Lent skeptic, for your encouragement to take this project on, and for your friendship. Bill and Annie Mahr, thank you for hosting me and Sam at Katalou this summer and for letting me write about your family mural. Ashley May, thank you for your professional-grade editorial help and feedback. Tim Brown, you were very kind to give me your ideas on leading children through Lent. Chris Castaldo, thank you for your insights on the chapter answering common objections.

Finally, I want to thank my family for their support. The love of my parents, Lou and Patti Damiani, has meant everything to me. Mom and Dad, thank you for your countless sacrifices on my behalf, for devoting yourselves to Jesus Christ, and for modeling the life of faith. Truly, I stand on your shoulders. To my in-laws, Ken and Sara Jo Gogots, your generosity and hospitality is a gift. Thanks for getting our family through the summer with ice cream sandwiches, swimming runs, and slumber parties. To my kids, Gus, Sam, Olivia, and Mona: I love you and am so proud to be your dad. Laura, thanks for your logical questions and loving heart. Your pilgrim soul keeps me humble and hopeful, and this book is dedicated to you.

Introduction

One day early in our engagement, my then-fiancée now-wife, Laura, and I were locked in a stalemate while sharing a Panera Bread "You Pick Two" lunch: where would we go to church once we were married?

It began politely enough but devolved into exasperation.

I wanted to find a church with great expository preaching and rich liturgy. Laura preferred a church with stirring worship and emotive stories of life-change.

"What's wrong with testimonies?" she asked me. "What's so bad about experiencing God's love in worship?"

Deciding on a church was much harder than ordering what lunch to share that day, and this time we could not "order" separately.

In a patronizing tone, I—a confident graduate student in theology—answered Laura's original question about what is wrong with testimonies in church: "The worship service is meant to exalt God, not humans. Testimonies should happen in small groups. There's already enough hype and individualism in American churches!"

I was so proud of my highly sophisticated religious palate—or so I thought. This conversation went nowhere. Week after week, we searched in vain to find the right church, and each experience gave us something new to critique.

Eventually a friend of ours recommended that we visit Church of the Resurrection, an Anglican church in the western suburbs of Chicago. I remember visiting the website for the first time and seeing a strange picture of people in robes standing behind a table with their arms reaching to the sky, smiling. *What kind of a church is this?* I thought.

We visited on the last Sunday of Epiphany, as the church was preparing for a journey we ourselves had never taken: the forty days of Lent. Without knowing why, we were drawn back to worship with them again, observing this strange communal practice like anthropologists visiting a foreign culture. *Don't all these rituals reflect a works-based understanding of salvation? What's the point of giving up the comforts of life? God doesn't need that from us!* Like many evangelicals who love the gospel, I had my doubts about Lent.

Yet, somehow, everyone we encountered who was practicing Lent seemed less burdened than I was. They appeared to be more joyful and satisfied, as if the Holy Spirit was working some magic on them. While I was preparing for my honeymoon, everyone around me was preparing for Easter. I had spent my extra money on a Caribbean cruise, while the weirdo Anglicans were freely giving their non-extra money to support the persecuted church in Jos, Nigeria. I was, admittedly, on the "Look Good Naked" diet, renouncing sweets for the sake of vanity. They were on the Good Friday diet, fasting from food to dwell more closely with Jesus Christ. I was feeding my cravings. They were confessing their sins. I was less obligated, but they were freer.

And no one was being pressured into Lent to make God or themselves happy. All were responding to a gracious, ancient invitation to walk with Jesus Christ in a tangible way for forty days. The people who said "Yes" to this invitation had only grace and joy for those of us who said "No" or "I'm not sure yet."

When I was finally ready to take the plunge, I learned that observing Lent is not a forced march of works-righteousness. But it was good medicine for my autonomy, self-indulgence, spiritual independence, and the painful split between what I knew about God and what I experienced of Him.

Laura and I went on that cruise after all. It was exciting at first, but its luster diminished every day. We ate at the chocolate bar. We bought souvenirs. We played mini golf. By the time we stepped off the ship, we concluded that it was not really worth the cost. Meanwhile, everyone in our new home church had been celebrating that Jesus had turned history inside out.

In the thirteen years since, we have not taken another cruise. But we keep returning to Lent—sometimes reluctantly, always imperfectly. Now that we have four small kids to lead through the season, it is more costly than ever. Yet every time we arrive at Easter Sunday, we always rejoice that it has been worth the cost, and then some.

I now pastor an Anglican church in Chicago filled with people who have little to no background in the cycles of the church calendar—the ancient way of ordering time around the life of Christ and His church, which includes Advent, Epiphany, Lent, Eastertide, and Pentecost. I frequently have conversations with Christians and spiritual seekers who feel drawn to walk with Christ through the practice of Lent but need to be taught the basics. This book is a result of those conversations.

Perhaps you're reading this because you feel drawn to the journey of Lent but want to know more. You are intrigued as you watch others you respect embrace this practice, yet you are interested to understand how it squares with your Protestant evangelical background. You might be wondering, *Is Lent a solitary practice, a communal practice, or both? How can I practice Lent if my church does not?* You have practical questions about what Lenten fasting, personal confession, and generosity might look like for you. This book is a primer to answer your questions and to get you started.

You might be a pastor or church planter seeking to know how to lead your congregation through Lent. You are not looking to switch denominations but want to appropriate this "mere Christian" practice—basic to Christians of all streams—in a way that fits your context. You would like to know the history, intention, and theological underpinnings of Lent in order to best inform your leadership and structure your preaching. You could use some advice for leading special services like Ash Wednesday, Palm Sunday, and Maundy Thursday. This book is for you.

Or you might be a Lent skeptic. Perhaps you're reading this because you have a family member or loved one who observes Lent and you want to understand them, even if you disagree with their convictions and practices. If that describes you, give special attention to part 1, which makes the case for Lent, and chapter 7 in particular, where I answer common objections to Lent.

Finally, this book is meant to be a pastor's encouragement to those who sense a call to deal with endemic spiritual disquiet and numbness in American evangelicalism. You love Jesus, but your passion has waned. You are sick of pretending to mourn on Good Friday and faking the joy on Easter. Perhaps you've hit a spiritual wall of some kind or feel the instability of our age and you need to rest in a larger, deeper, older practice that has stood the test of time. If that describes you, please keep reading. And know that I have been praying for you.

Part 1, "The Case for Lent," explores the biblical and historical basis for Lent and how it offers life to everyone seeking to follow Jesus. Chapters 1–7 discuss how Lent bonds us to Jesus Christ— His Word, His church, and His work. As we give up what we do not need, we gain Christ and our true selves in the process.

Part 2, "The Path of Lent," will guide you through the practicalities of Lenten fasting, prayer, and generosity (traditionally known as "almsgiving"). Since Lent is a season of gospel repentance, I have also included a chapter on how to make and hear confession of sin. And be sure not to skip chapter 12, "Tying It All Together," which is designed to help you connect all the dots and make a personalized plan for Lent based on God's work in your soul this year.

Part 3, "Leading Others through Lent," is designed for parents, pastors, and church leaders, and offers practical help for leadership, liturgy, and preaching in Lent. I will also share with you how Laura and I lead our children through this season. It is wonderfully meaningful for them as well.

Throughout I have included testimonies of ordinary people— some of whose names and circumstances have been changed for confidentiality—who have walked the journey of Lent, all of whom are imperfect but found their life in Christ changed during Lent. Yes, in the last thirteen years, I have come to appreciate the power of personal testimonies! And like the saints and fathers who have gone before me, I have learned that my wife is always right.

PART 1

THE
CASE
FOR
LENT

CHAPTER I

Into the Wilderness

We are not ready for Easter. Not emotionally, not spiritually.

But we always seem to be ready for the trappings of Easter.

For most Christians, Easter Sunday is a polite and happy occasion. Families, including mine, dress up in pastels and bow ties for the after-church picture. Children paint eggs, hunt for eggs, and consume Peeps and chocolate bunnies. We eat brunch, including delicious ham, and then move on with our lives.

Meanwhile, church leaders see Easter Sunday as an opportunity unlike any other to reach out to the community. Easter is still one of the highest-attended services of the year. As a local church pastor, I appreciate that people are open in a unique way on Easter Sunday. And I feel the pressure every year to preach a homerun sermon and to connect personally with spiritually curious visitors. The reality of church growth competes with Jesus' resurrection for my headspace and personal energy.

Despite all the hoopla and mixed motives, I believe pastors and parishioners alike sincerely want to celebrate Jesus' resurrection. You can sense the sincerity in the smiles, the sermons, and the earnest declarations of "He is risen!"—as well as in the half-startled responses of "He is risen indeed!" My experience before I practiced Lent was that this sincerity seemed to be somewhat forced. The attempts at celebration were often awkward. Easter Sunday is a victory feast, but in many churches it feels like a company picnic where everyone is expected to show up and be happy.

When Jesus Christ rose from the dead, history itself took a surprising, climactic turn. Even the people who had been preparing themselves for the reign of God could hardly believe it. To paraphrase Samwise Gamgee, Frodo's faithful companion in The Lord of the Rings, this meant that everything sad was coming untrue. Death itself had been turned on itself. Satan and his demons had run into the mousetrap of the cross, forfeiting their threats. And our Hero was making good on all His promises, sending His Spirit to renew the face of the earth, giving gifts as He ascended to His rightful throne.

It is the birthright of every Christian and gospel-proclaiming church to celebrate, feast, and exult in Jesus Christ on Easter Sunday. We are invited to participate in the stirring worship depicted in Revelation 4–5, giving honor and thanks with a loud voice to the Lion of the tribe of Judah. Every Sunday—and especially on Easter Sunday—we can overflow with hope every time we look upon Him whom we have pierced. He is not only seated on the throne, but is also healing our marriages, breaking our addictions, and uniting races and cultures into one family.

Christ has died! Christ is risen! Christ will come again! It is all true, gloriously so. Why, then, do we still feel awkward and halfhearted on Easter Sunday? In many cases, it's because our imaginations have been malnourished along the way to Resurrection Sunday. We have been secretly snacking on lesser stories—such as politics or our children's athletic success. In theory the gospel is compelling, but in reality we would rather pay attention to whatever Netflix is offering. We are so full on the junk food of our culture that we cannot metabolize the feast on our Easter plates.

Augustine had a phrase for this: *incurvatus in se*, meaning "curved in on oneself."[1] We were made to look upward and outward with our imaginations to behold the beauty of God in Christ. But like a Grand Canyon tourist who would rather look downward at his Instagram likes than outward at the breathtaking vistas in front of him, we have curved in on ourselves. We are called to worship, but we have chosen to fantasize. We have exchanged God's exhilarating and expansive story for lesser stories shaped by our fears, pain, and unhealthy desires.

The truth is that well before Easter, Jesus can wash, prepare, and fill our imaginations for worship. And this is where the practice of Lent comes in. But before I go further, I must tell you about Zorro.

Jumping into the Story

When I was growing up, my parents set aside Fridays as a family night. After dinner, our family of six would huddle around the TV and watch classic reruns. I was taken with *Zorro*, the show about a swashbuckling hero who confronted the corrupt, oppressive tyrants of 1820s California. Zorro was everything Batman was, except with an enviable mustache and peerless fencing skills.

I loved watching the nobleman Don Diego de la Vega transform himself into Zorro with a cape, mask, and wide-brimmed hat—all black. Zorro would inevitably find himself in a battle of wits and swords with evil men. After dominating them with his footwork and his horsewhip, he would leave a *Z* mark on their shirt with three swift movements of his sword. His enemies could only gape and curse in response.

I was so enthralled by Zorro that I wanted to jump inside the TV and become part of the story. But even more so, I wanted the story I was watching to jump outside the TV and transform my life. I wanted to become the type of person who could confront evil men and wield a sword like Zorro. So I started practicing with sticks from our backyard. Making the *Z* was tougher than it looked on TV! I remember asking my Dad to enroll me in fencing lessons. Zorro's story had captured my imagination to the extent that I wanted to live in it.

A compelling story has the effect of us wanting to participate, which is why my daughters want to become mermaids and my sons attend Hogwarts. And this, I believe, is why many Christians make, or aspire to make, a personal pilgrimage to the Holy Land. Walking the footsteps of Jesus allows them to tangibly inhabit His life and ministry. You can breathe the air of Bethlehem, be baptized in the Jordan River, and get your feet dusty on the road to Golgotha.

Perhaps you have heard the classic Holy Land testimony: "The Bible came alive for me!" I think such declarations communicate that salvation-history is not a spectator sport, but a vivid drama in which they participate.

Can you imagine taking a "Holy Land" pilgrimage every year in anticipation of Easter? This is the journey of Lent. Lent is an ancient pilgrimage that the Lord uses to recapture our imagination of and renew our participation in the greatest story ever told.

I doubt any Holy Land tour would take you to the wilderness for forty days. But perhaps they should. The desert is where God called his people to make them holy. We might assume that the wilderness is a place of exile and isolation, and it certainly can be that. But in the story of redemption, the wilderness has always been a sacred rendezvous spot for God and His beloved sons and daughters. In the wilderness, we detox from our false attachments and renew our sacred, primal bond with our loving Father.

Entering the Wilderness

When I am on a flight that is preparing for takeoff, I quietly defy the command to switch my electronic devices to airplane mode. Honestly, I chafe at this federal regulation. The plane will work just fine even if I send a few texts, right? I do not like airplane mode because it cuts me off from the stimulants and freedoms that I feel I need. It forces me to have an actual conversation with the person sitting next to me.

When God calls His people into the wilderness, He puts their whole existence on airplane mode. I resist this, and so might you. It means feeling out of control and out of the loop. Our go-to stimulants and stories are no longer on tap. We can no longer anesthetize our emotions. We can no longer avoid a conversation with our Father. It might feel like a restrictive punishment, but it's actually a heavenly gift. Lent is indeed a wilderness, and there are several reasons why we can and should enter it.

We enter the wilderness of Lent because the gospel is true. We do not go into the wilderness to find God. We enter the wilderness because God has found us. He has delivered us, blessed us, and called us His own. The desolation and quiet gives us space to ponder the great salvation we have already witnessed. Even our struggles and failures in the wilderness teach us the truth of the gospel.

Consider the people of Israel. They journeyed into the wilderness after watching their oppressors drown in the Red Sea by the hand of God. Exodus details the song of praise that carried them out of Egypt: "The Lord is my strength and my song, and he has become my salvation. . . . Pharaoh's chariots and his host he cast into the sea" (Ex. 15:2, 4).

The wilderness was not where Israel earned their salvation. It is where they internalized what it meant to be saved. In a desolate place, salvation came that shattered the earth. Bread fell from heaven; water gushed from a rock. The multitudes were fed by faith and with thanksgiving. The Living Word was in their midst, working beautiful and wild miracles, changing slaves into sons. With each nourishing meal, the tyranny and pretense of Egypt lost its grip. It took Israel forty years to realize they were the Lord's treasured possession, not Pharaoh's unworthy slaves.

Consider Jesus, true Israel. He entered the wilderness with his Father's baptismal endorsement ringing in His ears: "You are my beloved Son; with you I am well pleased" (Luke 3:22). Unlike Israel, and us, He had no false attachments of which to repent. His forty-day fast made space for Him to bask in His Father's love and to draw upon the Spirit's power. When the devil tempted Him with fantasies of dazzling self-love and godless power, Jesus was ready. He shut down the demonic chatter with the Word of God, which lived inside Him.

In the Lenten wilderness, our fantasies of glory, fear, or pleasure can give way to the reality of God's glory, love, and holiness. God acts in history, and we enter the wilderness to give our imaginations a chance to catch up.

We enter the wilderness of Lent to prepare for Easter. Why is Lent forty days?[2] Practically speaking, it takes at least that long to prepare our hearts for Easter. As Dallas Willard put it, "One drop of water every five minutes won't get you a shower."[3] We need to be immersed in the reality of the kingdom of God for big doses at a time before we start seeing its impact on our lives. The same is true for Easter Sunday—and the "Eastertide" Sundays that follow. We need more than a Good Friday service two days in advance to get into the state of mind and heart to celebrate Jesus' victory over death and hell. We cannot prepare for Easter over the weekend. No, we need to walk a longer pilgrimage to get ready.

Most importantly, the forty days draw us into the gospel drama that Jesus lived. He went into the wilderness before us, and He goes there again with us. He knows that the struggle is real, that our frame is weak, and that we are dust. Because we are united to Him, His forty days become ours.

We enter the wilderness to get to the Promised Land. Lent is not our ultimate destination. The wilderness fast is temporary, thanks be to God! The bright light of the resurrection is ahead. Can you see it? In fact, the word *Lent* derives from the old Saxon word for "spring," and Christians of Eastern traditions love to refer to the "Bright Sadness" that marks every Christian who will endure the darkness leading up to Easter.

In the Lenten Spring, winter is giving way to summer—life and sunrise and a great feast are ahead. Each day's light is longer than the last. Lent, then, is a profound picture of the Christian journey. It stands between our deliverance and our home. It is a time of faith and longing, hope and expectation.

No, we are not ready for Easter. Not yet. But with the world behind us and the cross before us, we go repenting and rejoicing one faltering step at a time. And everything sad is coming untrue.

CHAPTER 2

A (Mercifully Short) History of Lent

Where did Lent come from? How did it become recognized as the forty-day period of prayer, fasting, and generosity leading up to Easter? And when we say, "Lent began as a practice of the ancient church," what does that even mean?

To answer these questions, I invite you to picture yourself in a thorny pastoral situation. Imagine the Lord saw fit to answer your prayers for the unchurched, and revival broke out in your region of the Roman Empire. Your church is deluged with new converts, and the nets of your ministry are breaking from the surplus of fish reeled in by the gospel. People with broken pasts and no background in Christianity come readily to be filled with God's love in Christ. The poor and wealthy, young and old—people representing all the cultures of your region—are desperate to encounter Jesus and join His family.

It's the beautiful mess for which you've fasted and prayed. Now it's up to you to shepherd these sheep.

To complicate matters, imagine that Christianity is outlawed and branded as a public menace. State-controlled propaganda blames Christians for the Empire's various trials, and every weapon of the state and cultural elite is aimed at eradicating the worship of Jesus Christ. You meet secretly late at night or early in the morning, yet this leads the local officials to accuse you of conspiracy. Church leaders are often summoned and interrogated, sometimes tortured or even fed to beasts. Survivors sustain trauma, and so do you, since there is a price on your head. People crack under the pressure and renounce Christ for fear of losing family members, limbs, or their homes.

You have tough questions to answer, and the stakes for answering rightly could not be higher. For instance, who do you baptize and admit into your fellowship? A few of the "spiritual seekers" are likely state informants. How, then, do you discern one from the other? Others are hyped from their conversion but are ill-prepared for a life of cross-bearing. How do you bridge the gap?

Moreover, how do you maintain the integrity of the Christian faith while welcoming so many pagan converts? The church isn't growing incrementally; it's multiplying faster than you can keep track. And rival teachers are wooing the spiritually hungry with heretical teachings. You need a process of discipleship that is dynamic enough for the situation—and quick.

One more thing: Many who wavered under threat of torture want to be admitted back into fellowship. Others have brought scandal on themselves by committing murder or adultery, and they also want to be publicly forgiven. Though such people have not made unreasonable requests, they have broken faith with the family of God. Restoration should not happen without some kind of process.

How do you respond to these needs?

Binding Ourselves to Christ

The pastor-theologians of the church faced conditions like these in the first few centuries after Jesus' life and passion. And this is the environment out of which the practice of Lent emerged. Early church leaders called their people to devote themselves to a regular season of fasting, prayer, and almsgiving to form themselves as more mature Christians. This season later became known as Lent, but in the meantime it was simply a gentle harness that yoked the fledging church to Jesus Christ.

Fasting is a willing abstention from eating food, and some drinks, to make space in our souls to feast on Jesus. In short, fasting is "hunger for God, concretized."[1] For many people, this is the most painful *and* powerful part of Lent. We will cover the varieties of Lenten fasting in chapter 8.

Prayer is participating in the life of God, talking with and listening to Him, whether in solitude or communal worship. Christians pray using the Scriptures, especially the Psalms. In Lent, our prayers take on a tone of repentance and contrition, which we will discuss in chapter 9.

Almsgiving is a direct participation in God's generosity as we give away our resources in love to our neighbor. We'll look more closely at this in chapter 10.

When the Christian church weaves fasting, prayer, and almsgiving together over a period of several weeks, individuals, families, and communities are impacted powerfully. These practices strengthened the ancient church in at least four areas.

Spiritual growth. Seasons of prayer and fasting allowed our spiritual forebears to participate in their union with Jesus, who Himself fasted as He sought refuge in His Father's love

(Matt. 4:2). Jesus assumed that His followers would fast after he returned to the Father: "The days will come when the bridegroom is taken away from them, and then they will fast" (Matt. 9:15). Prayer and fasting were practical ways for the early church to receive Jesus' strength in their weakness.

Discipleship. Pagan converts to Jesus needed to cultivate new habits to support their walk with Christ. Fasting, prayer, and generosity over a period of time promoted spiritual reformation. Along the way, they received pastoral support in the form of prayer, fellowship, confession, and Bible teaching. In addition to forming new converts, this process helped to weed out informants.

Generosity. The early church took on responsibility for those marginalized by the Roman Empire, including abandoned babies, widows, lepers, and victims of plague. The practice of generosity, or almsgiving, made this sustainable. And when the early Christians fasted from food, they had more resources to give away.

Discernment. After persecution began to wane, many people who renounced Christ and betrayed their friends and family sought reentry into the church. Periods of fasting and prayer were integral to determining how and when to welcome apostates back into fellowship. Requiring the lapsed to fast, pray, and give generously helped to weed out the insincere.[2]

In short, Lenten practices were a loving and pastoral response to the needs of a congregation. And they still are, provided that we practice them in the right spirit.

Enrolling in Christ's School

But how did formal, prolonged practices that remind us of Lent become the season of Lent leading up to Easter?

The historical development of Lent is uneven and messy.[3] For three hundred years after Christ, different churches around the world took varying approaches to extended seasons of prayer, fasting, and generosity. Given the pace of growth and the heat of persecution, this is not surprising.

I am writing this chapter in the month of June, and my kids are still in school for another week. Chicago public schools usually begin class after Labor Day and end later in June, which offers both benefits and drawbacks. While my kids are finishing the school year, their cousins in Alaska, Texas, and Ohio are already enjoying summer break. But at the end of the day, my kids are learning the same subjects as their cousins. Yes, there are variations in the calendar, teaching styles, and local customs, but all the cousins are learning how to read, perform math equations, and dissect frogs.

As the early church wrestled with how to make disciples, they developed what we might consider "schools of Lent." They varied somewhat in timing and style, but they all had the same essential curriculum of Christ-centered prayer, fasting, and generosity. These church leaders would later develop universal standards that would stand the test of time. Three "schools of Lent" were most prominent during the first three hundred years of the church's life.

An intense baptism class. If you wanted to become a Christian under Roman persecution, you could enroll in a three-year process known as the "catechumenate," a full-immersion experience that taught the spiritually curious how to live, think, and worship as Christians before they were baptized and admitted into the complete fellowship of the church.[4] This often involved putting aside concubines, quitting professions that involved idolatry or injustice, and making restitution with people against whom one had sinned against by stealing, cheating, or deceiving. Those who had denied Christ in word or deed and wanted to rejoin the church could also enter the catechumenate. During the three years, candidates studied the Bible, attended worship services regularly, and received moral and theological instruction from their pastor. Once they had shunned their pagan ways and embraced the ways of Jesus, they were allowed to register for baptism. At that point, things got even more intense. Candidates and their sponsors—a more mature Christian who walked with them through the catechumenate process—would enter a three-week period of fasting and prayer. The fasting requirements of the catechumenate in part formed the basis of the Lenten fast in later centuries: one daily meal of vegetables. During the three-week fast, each candidate was interviewed, prayed over, and expected to memorize key doctrines of the Christian faith before they were baptized. In short, the catechumenate helped early Christians break old, sinful habits, reorder their loves, and conform their daily lives to the ways of Christ.

The Easter Fast. A few short years after Jesus' passion, the earliest Christians began to fast and pray to remember Jesus' death and celebrate His resurrection. As early as the first century, baptismal candidates and their sponsors fasted the day before Easter.[5] By the late second century, Christians fasted for forty hours, going without food and drink between the afternoon of Good Friday and the morning of Easter.[6] By the third century,

Christians fasted throughout Holy Week, and by the fourth century the Easter fast was extended to forty days.[7]

The Epiphany Fast. Whereas early Christians in North Africa and Rome fasted before their baptisms, those in Syria, Armenia, and Egypt practiced a forty-day fast after their baptisms. They sought to model Christ, who received His baptism and then spent forty days fasting in the desert. Epiphany is the season of the church calendar beginning in mid-January and celebrates the revelation of Christ's glory in His incarnation. Eastern Christians were enamored with Christ's glory and wanted to partake in Him, so they were baptized during Epiphany and then fasted after receiving the sacrament.[8]

While specific practices of each "school of Lent" were slightly different, they all shared the same rich gospel curriculum of humble repentance, spiritual renewal, and holy preparation for the mission of the church in the world. The early Christians were learning how to put their besetting sins to death ("mortification") and to experience new life in union with Christ ("vivification").

In the fourth century, the Roman Emperor Constantine converted to Christianity, and persecution of Christians eased considerably. This meant that Christian leaders could gather in safety, inform each other about the practices of their churches, and solidify their teachings. In 325, a diverse gathering of church leaders from around the world convened in Nicaea (in what is now modern Turkey) to decide on matters relating to theology and practice.

At this council, the church leaders decided that they all would practice Lent—they called it *Quadragesima*, meaning "fortieth" in Latin. They took the three overlapping fasts and turned them into one universal season leading up to the Easter feast. Yes, baptismal candidates would still fast, taking one simple meal in the evening, but now the whole church—every person in every region—was invited to join them.[9] Lent took the best parts of the catechumenate fast, the Easter Fast, and the Epiphany Fast and combined them into a universal, forty-day period that finds its culmination on Easter Sunday.

One of my friends who loves Jesus but is skeptical of Lent once asked me, "If Lent and Easter are so wonderful, why just celebrate them once a year?" This is a great question, and history shows that Christians in Rome insisted that every Friday is a "little Lent" and that every Sunday is a "little Easter." As such, Sundays are for feasting and rejoicing in Christ, not fasting.[10] So in 487, the church excluded Sundays from the forty days of Lent. That's why Lent begins on Ash Wednesday, to account for all forty days.[11]

Even though Lent became a standard season for the Christian church in the fourth century, it has always been flexible enough to adjust to the local culture and pastoral needs of the people. Fasting, prayer, and generosity are woven together differently for Christians in different parts of the world. Even in my own life, Lent is never quite the same each time I practice it.

But the pastoral vision for this season remains unchanged: Lent is a school that trains people to live as Christians. It is so effective at forming us into the likeness of Christ that we continue it to this day.

CHAPTER 3

Repeating History—
the Right Way

My friends Annie and Bill decided to do some bold decorating in their dining room. On one wall they painted a mural of their family history. I'm not talking about the history of just their lives, their parents' lives, or even their grandparents' lives. That's all included, but the mural also includes events from hundreds of years ago. Messy situations, controversial events, blunders, swindles, and lynchings—stuff the rest of us would want to sweep under the rug, not display on our dining room walls.

One panel shows Annie's ancestor Jack Horner, crouching in shame outside a beautiful estate he allegedly stole from a Catholic bishop. Henry VIII rewarded ole Jack for his treachery, but history disgraced him for it. Perhaps you've heard the old nursery rhyme about Little Jack Horner who "stuck in his thumb and pulled out a plum, and said, 'What a good boy am I!'" Yikes. That's Grandpa.

Another panel is pure contradiction. It pictures the beautiful estate of Annie's great-grandfather, Bibb, a well-loved Baptist preacher and man of God. It all seems good, except that his estate has slaves working in the fields. And he was a Confederate spy. Not exactly a great conversation piece when guests come over.

Why on earth would Bill and Annie display all this in their own home? In Annie's words, "I decided to let it stand as a cautionary tale to me not to ever forget how much the cultural norms can influence me, and how dependent on the mercy of God I am." In part, Bill and Annie had that mural painted to know what they were capable of. It is a spiritual history of their family—the good, the bad, the ugly.

Everyone in God's family has a spiritual history, extending back to the garden of Eden. It's messy yet covered with God's mercy. As you consider practicing Lent, I want to paint a mural of sorts that captures major themes from our family history. Together we'll walk through one scene at a time. Unless we see what we are capable of, we might dive headfirst into Lent and repeat history in a way we never intended. Or we might dismiss Lent outright and make the opposite error of reckless self-indulgence.

The Hunger Strike

The first panel is filled with images of pious people who are fasting, praying, and even acting generously with their possessions—all classic Lenten disciplines, mind you. If you get close to the wall, you can see that their expressions are serious and somber. And a little angry.

It's a hunger strike.

At its heart, a hunger strike is a power play. It's one of the last cards you can throw down as a prisoner, political dissident, or slave. The point is to fast in order to force the hand of the higher-ups to satisfy your demands. It's a high-stakes move. Once you go on hunger strike and a few others join you, the game changes, or at least that's the intention.

Hunger strikes are about power, not love. And that's how some of our forefathers related to God. They acknowledged His influence and tried to manipulate Him. So they went without food, put on sackcloth and ashes, and waited for God to meet their demands. But God does not play games with us. He is not enticed by our bribes, impressed with our asceticism, or cowed by our manipulations.

The sad, angry people in the hunger strike panel are all screaming in unison:

> Why have we fasted, and you see it not?
> Why have we humbled ourselves, and you take no
> knowledge of it? (Isa. 58:3)

And,

> It is vain to serve God. What is the profit of our keeping
> his charge or of walking as in mourning before the
> Lord of hosts? (Mal. 3:14)

When we meet God's commands in hope that He will meet our demands, we think we are high-functioning, pious people. We are showing God how serious we are. "I'm fasting so God will bring revival to this city," "so my son will return to the Lord," "to show God I'm ready to meet my spouse," or, "so God will take this temptation away."

By all appearances, we look spiritual, so earnest. But like our ancestors, eventually we will fall and be bitterly disappointed. The elder brother in Jesus' parable about the Prodigal Son said to his father, "Look, these many years *I have served you*, and I never disobeyed your command, yet *you never gave me a young goat*, that I might celebrate with my friends" (Luke 15:29, emphasis added). His faithfulness to his father wasn't motivated by love, but by swag. "I served you for your goats! Where are my goats, Dad?" This is cold reciprocity laid bare. The fictional elder brother was miserable and gloomy, like the real-life Pharisees he personified.

The hunger strike scene pictures a miserable circus. Religious people jump through pointless hoops. They whip their own flesh to the point of bleeding. Everyone tries to out-suffer others in order to merit God's intervention. This is the spiritual sickness behind the medieval practice of indulgences. Yet, there are Christians of every stripe and era in this panel, including us Protestants. All of us are capable of self-obsession that knows nothing of the original vision for Lent or Christian discipleship.[1]

Martin Luther and his fellow Reformers were right to protest the way Lent was practiced in their day. It had become a hunger strike *par excellence*. Lent had become a clearinghouse for religious corruption and control.

Take a good look at this first panel. This is in our ancestry, and it is only by God's mercy that we ourselves are not painted in it. Heaven forbid that our Lenten practices turn us into judgmental, arrogant cranks. We are wise to remember Paul's admonition to the church in Galatia:

> O foolish Galatians! Who has bewitched you? It
> was before your eyes that Jesus Christ was publicly
> portrayed as crucified. . . . Did you receive the Spirit
> by works of the law or by hearing with faith? Are you
> so foolish? Having begun by the Spirit, are you now

being perfected by the flesh? . . . Does he who supplies
the Spirit to you and works miracles among you do so
by works of the law, or by hearing with faith—just as
Abraham "believed God, and it was counted to him as
righteousness"? (3:1–3, 5–6)

We are not justified by fasting, prayer, and generosity. Nor are
we justified by expository preaching, social justice, or reciting the
Sinner's Prayer correctly. We are justified by grace through faith.
Thanks be to God! There is a place for Lent and its disciplines, so
long as we don't see them as means for a hunger strike.

The All-Inclusive Resort

The next panel is much different. Behold, the all-inclusive resort.
This resort is filled with those who are fed up with the sancti-
mony of the hunger strike. Here the people of God overindulge
every appetite of the body. Adam and Eve are in the center. Their
mouths are open, their hands outstretched—not for praying, but
for gorging. They fill their bellies and forget about God.

This resort is not family-friendly. Don't let your kids look
at it, unless you let them read the Old Testament. Because the
children of Israel are depicted acting extravagantly next to their
golden calf—eating, drinking, and rousing (Ex. 32:6).

This first panel looks a lot like a spring-break trip, a frat party,
a free-for-all. It's where we find the Prodigal Son, squandering
his money and living recklessly (Luke 15:13). Everyone is going
back for seconds and thirds—for whatever they want. This is for
everyone who has been liberated from "religion," for whom "all
things are lawful" (1 Cor. 10:23).

The idea of an all-inclusive resort is that you pay one lump sum for full access. But who is paying the lump sum in this panel? It's not who you think.

If you look carefully, you'll see our spiritual ancestors trampling on others, specifically the poor, to get what they wanted. Jacob is taking Esau's blessing to get ahead. Judah and his brothers are selling Joseph for some cash. The Israelites of Judges 21 are ambushing foreign dancers to make them their wives. King David is using his power to bed Bathsheba and kill her husband, Uriah. The wealthy Corinthian church members are indulging while the less-wealthy members go hungry. When we give way to excess, injustice follows close behind.

Ezekiel called out the spiritual leaders of Israel who used their power to feed themselves rather than to care for those entrusted to their authority:

> Ah, shepherds of Israel who have been feeding
> yourselves! Should not shepherds feed the sheep?
> You eat the fat, you clothe yourselves with the wool,
> you slaughter the fat ones, but you do not feed the
> sheep. (Ezek. 34:2–3)

The all-inclusive resort is a story of the haves and have-nots. Many of the women and children are exploited financially or otherwise. Only a few people are having fun: mostly powerful men.

But everybody is degraded. Everyone is serving an appetite, theirs or someone else's. Painted above the debauched images are the grave words of the apostle Paul: "Their end is destruction, their god is their belly, and they glory in their shame, with minds set on earthly things" (Phil. 3:19).

As one who lives in an American city with access to every

pleasure imaginable, the all-inclusive resort is not far from home. In Chicago, almost any craving can be satisfied—cheaply, secretly. GrubHub can supply the food, Saucey can deliver the alcohol, and Tinder can get you sex. Maybe you just want to be entertained. Jump on a peer-to-peer video console, an adult website, or Amazon Prime Video.

For those of us living in the affluent West, embedded into our daily lives is the implicit belief that it's crazy to deny your appetites. And giving way to this belief is like riding on a lazy river. Unless you swim upstream, it will take you places you never imagined. Just ask my friend Vince.

When I met Vince, his marriage was in danger due to his pornography addiction. Even though he grew up in the church and had a strong faith in Christ, he was never quite able to master his addiction, which began in junior high. So instead of starving his cravings, he fed them secretly. His hunger for sexual pleasure, good food, and comfort were never tamed, until it wrecked his sexual union with his wife and his capacity to feel strong emotions. It was my joy to walk Vince through a process of gospel restoration, which included the intentional denial of his cravings. I saw Vince discover and express the freedom Christ offers anyone who will surrender their appetites to Him.

Some of us are suspicious of Lent because choosing hunger seems like senseless self-injury. "We're free in the gospel!" some say. "God doesn't need our fasting!" Yes and amen. But beware: the ambient culture has confused the meaning of *freedom*, which no doubt affects the way many of us understand it.

In the Scriptures, Jesus is the Lord who sets us free to love God and neighbor. Fasting helps us participate in that freedom. But in the modern West, pleasure is the "lord" who is said to set us free to consume our neighbor—and God, for that matter.

Does "free in the gospel" mean that we never fast, something that every single Protestant Reformer practiced and taught, whether or not they advocated for Lent?

Let's look at one last panel.

A Table in the Wilderness

My favorite scene in Bill and Annie's mural is the one depicting "rescue." In this scene, Annie is a little girl playing in the creek with her granny who saved her life when she was practically orphaned. Her husband, Bill, who would save her from self-destruction as an adult, approaches the creek from a distance. In the shadow of this mural, I have witnessed Annie and Bill repeat this story of rescue time and again as they provide spiritual care and hospitality to people who feel weary and lost. I see them care for her special-needs granddaughter with the same tenderness depicted in the mural. I see them engage and pray over my son Sam, their godson.

This rescue panel is three-dimensional. It has a living quality to it. The mural doesn't just remind them of what they are *capable of*; it speaks to what they are *called to* in Christ so that she and her family can repeat history the right way.

What are we called to?

The final panel in our Lenten mural is a table in the wilderness. Here in the desert, Jesus sits at a table set for Him by His Father. His head is anointed with oil, and His countenance is bright. Though He's fasting from physical nourishment, He's feasting on His Father's love. He masters His physical appetite and metabolizes the bread, which is not bread. Like the poet of Psalm 23, Jesus is surrounded by enemies, wild animals, and Satan himself. But He's filled with the Word of God. The Holy Spirit leads him, and angels minister to him. This table is nothing less than heaven breaking into earth.

In his scene, Jesus does not simply feast on God. He *is* a feast for hungry people. He is the Bread of Heaven, broken for the life of the world. All who eat of Him will never hunger, and all who drink of Him will never thirst (John 6:35). Above this mural reads an invitation from the prophet Isaiah:

> Come, everyone who thirsts,
> come to the waters;
> and he who has no money,
> come, buy and eat!
> Come, buy wine and milk
> without money and without price. (Isa. 55:1)

Sitting on Jesus' left are all those faithful Israelites who fasted and prayed in anticipation of the Messiah: Moses, Elijah, and everyone else who believed the Law and the Prophets. On His right are all those He taught to fast and pray: the disciples, the apostles, and everyone else who is alive in Christ. Refugees from the hunger strike and the all-inclusive resort have found their way and are also seated at the table. And they look relieved. On their faces you can see a look of long-awaited satisfaction. Jesus is helping them unlearn the lie that God demands our merit, or that God is a magic vending machine. The Lord is their Shepherd, and they shall not want.

As this fellowship fills up on God's generosity, it begins to overflow from them to others. Compassion for the poor and the persecuted naturally follow. Justice rolls down like waters.

The resources of the fellowship are directed outward to feed the hungry, clothe the naked, and care for the sick. Slaves are becoming sons, broken people are getting healed, and those who had been debased are made holy unto the Lord. The gathering is marked by repentance, salvation, and freedom. Every appetite is eventually set in order.

So many are seated at the table. As I begin to count them, I find they are more than the sand of the seashore, more than the stars in the sky. They all seem to shine like stars, but no one as brightly as the Son. This panel makes me squint, but I can't look away.

Finally, I find that the faces are looking back at me, looking back at you. Their faces pose a joyful invitation: "Won't you come join us?"

> Therefore, since we are surrounded by so great a cloud of witnesses, let us also lay aside every weight, and sin which clings so closely, and let us run with endurance the race that is set before us, looking to Jesus, the founder and perfecter of our faith, who for the joy that was set before him endured the cross, despising the shame, and is seated at the right hand of the throne of God. (Heb. 12:1–3)

A cloud of witnesses invites us to feast on Jesus through fasting, prayer, and generosity. Along with Jesus, they are cheering for us to sit at the table. To do so may mean that we lay aside some comfortable hindrances, that we say goodbye to a few attachments. "Good riddance. I want a seat next to Jesus at the table!" This is what I'm called to. And so are you.

When we practice Lent in the spirit of Jesus, it's not about making God happy, looking spiritual, or repeating empty traditions. It's not a power move or a forced march. Jesus and the cloud of witnesses show us that Lent is about Jesus— and, therefore, about love. The Holy Spirit uses fasting, prayer, and generosity to satisfy us with God's fatherly love. As a result, we are moved to share that love with others. And that is history worth repeating.

CHAPTER 4

Receiving the Humility of Christ

You Are Beautiful.

This simple message has blanketed the city of Chicago through murals, graffiti, large installations, and tiny stickers on lampposts. As you get on the "L", exit Lake Shore Drive, or walk through the Loop, you will eventually be reminded that you are beautiful. When I walk my kids to the local park, we see "YOU ARE BEAUTIFUL" displayed in life-sized letters draped on the side of the gate.

I cannot believe people went through all that trouble for me, and I'm flattered every time I see the message. I appreciate the intention of the artists behind this campaign: "We want to make life a little better . . . by grabbing strangers unexpectedly in the grind of their daily life, and unapologetically saying it's OK to be human."[1] It's true that people everywhere are burdened by a sense of their own worthlessness. I'm sure some have been encouraged for a moment by this announcement, but at the end of the day, self-affirmations cannot heal self-hatred.

But it's not from a lack of trying.

Beyond its use as a public art campaign, "You are beautiful" can also be seen as a creed for our cultural moment. The full text of the creed might read something like:

You are beautiful.
You are spectacular.
You are a rock star.
Your dreams are sacred,
The universe is trying to help you
And the universe is inside you.
So stop hating yourself
And show the world who you are.
Believing this creed is the same thing
As believing in yourself.

I don't know which is heavier: the burden of self-hatred or that of self-blessing. It seems that our churches are filled with people who are crushed by both. On one shoulder, they carry shame that their dreams haven't come true. They hoped for something and got burned. They have failed to change the world and gain glory in the process. And as they age, they feel less attractive, less invincible. Mortality and gravity start pulling them down—slowly. Whereas previous generations felt guilty, many of us are wallowing in shame, feeling unworthy of love.

On the other shoulder, they carry the responsibility to affirm themselves. "I'm beautiful, even if I'm balding." "My life plan is sacred, even though it has left me bankrupt." "I must assert myself, express myself, mustering confidence from deep within." But what happens when the confidence runs out?[2]

It's strange, really. Building people up in the wrong way can end up crushing them. Yes, we need encouragement, love, and empathy our whole lives. Most people don't get enough of that. But we don't need to be the epicenter of reality, worshiping ourselves and demanding others to join in. That will only make us self-involved. We will be ill-equipped to suffer well, to grow from negative feedback, and to put others ahead of ourselves. That is no way to live.

If everyone is awesome, who does the dishes? Who goes last in the grocery store line? Who among us is strong enough to spend our best years caring for the elderly and disabled? Who has the security to offer a gentle answer in response to an angry insult? We are epic, amazing, beautiful people who throw fits when our will is crossed. We brag "humbly" on social media, and avoid menial tasks. All this self-worship detracts from the greater good. Families, institutions, and communities by nature challenge us to lay aside our individual pursuits for the common good. All three require humble self-sacrifice and an honest perception of reality. And all three are disintegrating before our eyes.

Lent is good medicine for individuals and the communities they inhabit. It is a season for us to receive the humility of Christ in such a way that frees us to pour ourselves out in love toward others. This happens in three ways: (1) The *ashes* of Lent reorient us to reality; (2) the *limits* of Lent diminish our power; and (3) the *Lord* of Lent displays the true beauty of downward mobility.

The Ashes of Lent

For thousands of years, the human race operated under the assumption that the earth was the center of the universe. Though a delusion, it must have felt like a wonderful compliment. The sun dutifully encircles us with its light. The planets waltz for the delight of the human race. The stars and heavenly bodies align themselves in just the right way so that we could receive special messages about reality. The universe was about us, and we were flattered.

In the 1500s, Polish astronomer Nicolaus Copernicus started making some troubling observations. Celestial bodies don't exactly revolve around a single point. The earth seems to be the one spinning and rotating around the sun, not the other way around. The earth appears to be a lot closer to the sun than it is to the stars. At some point the penny drops for Copernicus: We aren't at the center of the universe—not even close. Tycho Brahe, Johannes Kepler, and Galileo Galilei would eventually confirm and refine his observations. Their discoveries were sobering. The idea that the earth and sun were switching places made people angry and depressed. Seventeenth-century Anglican poet John Donne channeled the anguish of the day in his poem "Anatomy of the World":

> And new philosophy calls all in doubt,
> The element of fire is quite put out,
> The sun is lost, and th'earth, and no man's wit
> Can well direct him where to look for it.
> And freely men confess that this world's spent,
> When in the planets and the firmament
> They seek so many new; they see that this
> Is crumbled out again to his atomies.
> 'Tis all in pieces, all coherence gone.

The Copernican Revolution was a humbling reality check. But who would want to go back? It's better for the human race to be in touch with reality. While emotionally disorienting, the revolution helped redirect our awe away from ourselves to the grandeur of God, where it belongs. We may not be at the center of the universe, but we exist for the pleasure of a loving God who holds together all things by the word of His power (Col. 1:15–20; Heb. 1:3).

Lent is like an annual Copernican Revolution. The season begins with the Ash Wednesday service, which is designed to reorient us to reality. The minister smears ashes in the shape of a cross on the forehead of every man, woman, and child, and says, "Remember that you are dust, and to dust you shall return" (see Gen. 3:19).[3] To reinforce the point further, it is customary to receive these ashes while kneeling.[4]

We are not invincible. We are not self-sufficient. And we are not at the center of the universe—not even close. As the ashes are pressed onto our foreheads, we remember that apart from grace we are but dust, not demigods. The ancients may have been mistaken about the earth's place in the universe, but they were rightly aware of our finitude. Here is a sample reading from the Ash Wednesday service as prescribed by *The Book of Common Prayer*:

> As for man, his days are like grass;
> he flourishes like a flower of the field;
> for the wind passes over it, and it is gone,
> and its place knows it no more.
> (Ps. 103:15–16)

On one level, our days are numbered, and we will surrender everything we have spent a lifetime accumulating: our careers, possessions, freedoms, closest relationships, and our body. The ashes of Lent won't let us forget this. On another level, however, our lives are hidden with Christ in God (Col. 3:1–4). God "knows our frame; he remembers that we are dust" (Ps. 103:14). By God's mercy, we have a great future in His kingdom long after our bodies fail us. God has everything, God *is* everything, and in Christ we are forever united with God! This hope is symbolized by the fact that the ashes take the shape of the cross. The Anglican prayer for Ash Wednesday captures wonderfully this tension:

> Almighty God, you have created us out of the dust of the earth: Grant that these ashes may be to us a sign of our mortality and penitence, that we may remember that it is only by your gracious gift that we are given everlasting life; through Jesus Christ our Savior. Amen.[5]

Being at the center of the universe is a burden too heavy for our shoulders. Beginning on Ash Wednesday, Lent opens us up to the divine blessing that we can receive only when our hands are empty and we no longer see ourselves at the center. We might be dust, but we have the cross, and that is more than enough.

The Limits of Lent

The practices of Lent limit our earthly power. I feel this every time I fast. How am I supposed to lead a staff meeting when I have a headache? How does a sermon get written when my stomach is growling? Generosity leaves us with fewer resources, especially money, which we often use strictly for ourselves. Prayer requires attention and time we would normally give toward controlling situations. In short, the arm of our will is shortened in Lent, and that is good.

My friend Megan discovered this firsthand. She was four days into a familiar Lenten fast of sweets, which was, by her own admission, "more to whittle my waistline than to draw near to my Savior." She was surprised on the fifth day by a strong conviction from the Lord to give up her makeup. "At that point in my life (I was twenty) it was one of the hardest things I'd ever done. It was a time when I was very appearance-focused, and I obsessed all day long about how I looked." Megan realized that while makeup itself was not bad, her relationship to makeup had become a tool for securing her identity in the eyes of others.

As Megan put away all her powders and brushes and "walked into the world bare-faced for the rest of Lent," she was confronted with her diminished power. The arm of her will was shortened as she surrendered the power that came with a perfect appearance. "I hated it at first," she admits, "as people kept saying, 'You look different,' and 'You look so tired.'" But as Megan offered up this state of weakness to Jesus, "He began to cultivate in me an inner beauty through growth in Him. If my hands were clutching lip gloss or mascara, I couldn't have received that heavenly gift."

As Megan's earthly power diminished, her spiritual freedom increased and her relationship to makeup was reordered. She told me, "This process of focusing on Christ and cultivating my inner beauty over my outward appearance is a countercultural endeavor, especially for a woman in our airbrushed, Photoshop-obsessed Western society. Because of that, it is still a journey and something I have to work at almost every day."

What do you use to control situations, to feel accepted, and to have your will accomplished? In Lent, you may sense a call, like Megan did, to give up something that makes you feel powerful. If so, pursue it with prayer, fasting, and generosity. Limiting our food, purchases, and other things dear to us will give the Lord ample opportunity to be strong in our weakness.

But for many of us who have additional powers unknown to other generations, we might add other items to the list: social media, gaming, shopping for luxuries, or screens altogether. You might even choose to give away business to a competitor.[6] When Jesus fasted and prayed for forty days, the Father gave Him the strength to resist the temptation to gain power (Matt. 4:1–11).

The Lord of Lent

Roger Brandt is a lifelong family friend. We used to live down the street from Roger and his family in Kettering, Ohio. A veteran of the Air Force, Roger was the closest thing to a rocket scientist I ever met. He held advanced degrees in electrical engineering, taught astrodynamics at the Air Force Academy, and tested GPS technology for the Air Force before the technology was mainstream. But I didn't know any of that until doing research for this book, because Roger never mentioned it. He was too busy taking my sisters and me out for ice cream, letting us run around his house, or helping my dad with household repairs. He was like a big brother to my parents and a grandfather to us kids.

One fateful day, our 1971 Volkswagen Squareback was inadvertently filled with diesel fuel instead of regular. We didn't have the tools we needed, so my parents called Roger. With an encouraging smile on his face, Roger attached an old-fashioned siphoning hose to the fuel tank, bent down, and sucked the diesel fuel out of the engine. As you can imagine, some of the diesel got in his mouth as he initiated the reverse flow of the fuel.

What would compel one of the most accomplished men we knew to take fuel into his mouth with no angle other than to serve? Simply put, Roger loved our family. And Roger loved us because he knew he was loved by God. It was as if Roger was loaded up with so much love that he couldn't help but descend. Love sinks us down to the place where we can serve.

An eighteenth-century French mystic likened humility to a sea vessel being weighed down by a stabilizing mass:

> As when we load a vessel, the more ballast we put in,
> the lower it sinks; so the more love we have in the soul,
> the lower we are abased in self. . . . Let its depths be
> made known by our readiness to bear the cross.[7]

Ships without a load are too flimsy to last on the open waters. Without enough ballast—heavy material like sandbags or lead—weighing the vessel down, the choppy waters and stormy weather would make quick work of any ship. The more ballast, the lower the ship sinks into the water. The lower the ship sinks into the water, the more secure it becomes, and the farther it is able to travel.

Such is the humility of Jesus. The more of His Father's love that He took on board, the lower He sank into the water. No one was more full of God's love, no one was more willing to become a servant of all, and no one was more secured for His mission.

> Jesus, knowing that the Father had given all things into
> his hands, and that he had come from God and was
> going back to God, rose from supper. He laid aside his
> outer garments, and taking a towel, tied it around his
> waist. Then he poured water into a basin and began
> to wash the disciples' feet and to wipe them with the
> towel that was wrapped around him. (John 13:3–5)

Can you see Jesus sinking down to wash feet, full of His Father's blessing? When we seek to bless ourselves, we avoid anything but promotions. But when we read passages like John 13 and Philippians 2, we see that experiencing the love of God, and knowing who we are in Christ, drives us downwards. Jesus' stature before the Father freed Him to descend to self-emptying, servanthood, humiliation, and death.

Orthodox pastor and writer Alexander Schmemann reminds us that "God himself is humble!"[8] After inhaling the smog of obnoxious celebrities for so long, it's refreshing to ponder the beautiful humility of Jesus. He didn't push, pretend, or throw fits to fulfill His mission. He was always gracious under pressure, took on menial tasks, and even forgave His enemies. The Lord of glory was and is humble. He's praying without ceasing for us right now, and He's weeping, rejoicing, and serving with His saints around the world.

Jesus didn't come to be served, and He still doesn't.

Would you like to exchange the burden of self-obsession for the easy yoke of Jesus' humility? This is one of the chief reasons to observe Lent. It's a humbling experience in the best sense. Jesus is waiting for you to sink down with Him.

> When I see the King of Glory
> giving up
> advantages I've wanted my whole life,
> from infancy to carpentry
> a human,
> washed by John
> filled with a Spirit
> speaking my language—
> Father's love in His eyes, descending
> to the depths,

touching boils and heels
plunged into a Lake of Horrors
held under by that tenderness
for daughters and sons
He does not despise,
raised to rule
raised to serve
always a Gardener
I can only say in response,
You Are Beautiful.

CHAPTER 5

Confessing Our Secrets

In 2010, our family survived "Snowmageddon," a blizzard that blanketed Washington, D.C., in thirty inches of snow. It took several weeks for the city to clear the streets of the white stuff. As a result, the garbage trucks could not drive into the alleys to collect the garbage cans. For weeks, our refuse piled up, the cans overflowing with flimsy plastic bags containing dirty diapers and rotting food. And because of the snow, we couldn't take the cans to the alley, so the trash pile was right outside our door. It became a feast for the rats and a scourge for the humans. After a while, we began to dread walking outside our back door.

One day it dawned on me: *garbage collectors are my heroes.* I produce waste every day, and I need someone to take it away— forever. Otherwise it slowly imprisons me in my own home. I am burdened and helpless unless someone can remove my garbage.

After some of the neighbors had shoveled a rough path into our alley, something wonderful happened. I was doing some work at home when I heard a beautiful sound outside the window: the beep-beep of the garbage truck. Before it was too late, I raced down the stairs, flung open the back door, and ran toward the garbage truck with a bag of refuse in each hand. "Can you take these from me?" I asked breathlessly.

What a relief it was to cast my burdens onto the garbage collectors! They took every bag.

We can draw a parallel to our spiritual lives. In the course of our life, we accumulate a different kind of waste. It is less tangible, but just as real—and lethal. We might call it toxic waste for the soul: shameful moments, destructive patterns, and tragic choices. Some of the garbage is inherited: Our parents or grandparents dumped the waste onto our lawn before we knew what was happening. And now their legacy of alcoholism or anxiety—you name it—lives on in us. Some of our garbage is chosen: the secret vice, the string of words that escaped our lips, the police record that can't go away. Much of our garbage is communal: we have created refuse piles towering to the heavens, and we add to them in our own individual way, whether it's racial animosity, economic greed, or sexual exploitation.

We don't just need a hero to remove our physical garbage. We need one who can take away our spiritual garbage. Whether we inherited it or chose it, it clings to our memories, it poisons our relationships, and it weighs us down. If there was such a garbage collector, who came not to condemn us for our trash but to take it away forever, we would no doubt rejoice. And we need a hero who can take every bag.

The Lamb of God who takes away the sin of the world—His death for us on the cross is the only solution for our toxic waste. That remedy is available to anyone, anytime. All we need to do is humbly and repentantly cry, "Jesus Christ, Son of God, have mercy on me!" and He will immediately answer that prayer with His forgiveness and cleansing.

We need Lent because repentance is not just a prayer. It is a posture. We need time and space to become repentant people, to experience the depths of Jesus' forgiveness. Our default posture is to use Jesus' forgiveness like we use the car wash: as a fast, convenient solution to a surface problem. The truth is that the cleansing process needs to go much deeper, like a thorough spring cleaning. It cannot be rushed.

Lent provides forty days for us to behold Christ and His cross, not only to understand it more deeply, but also to cast our soul's toxic waste upon it. I invite you to imagine Lent as a season when Jesus heals and restores what sin has destroyed in our souls, families, and congregations. The sermons, silence, and ancient prayers of confession during Lent all teach us a posture of gospel repentance.

Perhaps you've always thought of Lent as a substitute for the cross of Christ, where instead of looking to Jesus we turn to ourselves—to our ashes, somberness, and sacrifices—to pay for our own sin. But that's not what Lent is about. Lent is a ministry of Christ's cross that brings healing and freedom. Practicing Lent is like taking a long bath in the wonderful grace of Jesus. I have experienced it, and so have countless others.

False substitutes for the cross of Christ abound. Lent isn't one of them. The most deadly substitute is secrecy. Satan, the enemy of our souls, suggests to us that we cannot afford to let our sin—or the sins of others committed against us—to be exposed. He shames us into burying the toxic waste in the backyard and pretending it doesn't exist. Satan loves it when we self-loathe in secret. He hates the cross and the forgiveness available to us when sin is unearthed and confessed.

Secrecy is the steroid of sin, intensifying its power to destroy us. In the words of the psalmist, "When I kept silent, my bones wasted away through my groaning all day long" (Ps. 32:3). And

Dietrich Bonhoeffer notes,

> Sin demands to have a man by himself. The more
> isolated a person is, the more destructive will be
> the power of sin over him, and the more deeply he
> becomes involved in it, the more disastrous is his
> isolation. Sin wants to remain unknown. It shuns the
> light. In the darkness of the unexpressed it poisons the
> whole being of the person.[1]

By attempting to save ourselves through secrecy, we cut ourselves off from Jesus' loving grace. Hiding our sin is hell on earth! It alienates us from God, our community, and our true selves. Imagine the long-term impact of burying toxic waste under your home instead of disposing of it properly. Everything might look functional on the outside, but the toxicity underneath would work a quiet destruction.

Jesus invites us to give Him all of our toxic waste, to send it to His cross. He wants us to be free. The season of Lent ministers Christ's freedom because it makes space for sin to be identified, confessed, and healed.

How Sin Is Identified

Sin is identified in the liturgy of Christian worship. Liturgy means "the work of the people," and Christian liturgy is a series of scripturally based prayers that proclaim the gospel and help us participate in it. As a pastor, I have found that beautiful liturgy can take the pressure off me and the congregation as we worship together. Taking up ancient prayers gives us freedom to respond with joy and unity to God's work on our behalf. Even "nonliturgical" churches have a liturgy: they invite some kind of structured, meaningful participation in worship of the triune God.

Christian liturgy animated by the power of the Holy Spirit is as interactive as it gets, shaping body and soul, reordering loves and desires.[2] No matter what tradition you belong to, you can use ancient prayers and readings to lead your congregation to renewed repentance and faith in the finished work of Christ.

At Immanuel Anglican Church, the congregation I pastor in Chicago, we open our Ash Wednesday service with a prayer that honors the Lord's inclination to forgive as well as His power to help us confess our sins:

> Almighty and everlasting God, you hate nothing you
> have made and forgive the sins of all who are penitent:
> Create and make in us new and contrite hearts, that
> we, worthily lamenting our sins and acknowledging our
> wretchedness, may obtain of you, the God of all mercy,
> perfect remission and forgiveness; through Jesus Christ
> our Lord, who lives and reigns with you and the Holy
> Spirit, one God, for ever and ever. Amen.[3]

After an invitation to enter the season of self-examination and repentance, we name the sins that ensnare every generation:

> We have not loved you with our whole heart, and
> mind, and strength. We have not loved our neighbors
> as ourselves. We have not forgiven others, as we have
> been forgiven. We have been deaf to your call to serve,
> as Christ as served us. . . .
> We confess to you, Lord, all our past unfaithfulness:
> the pride, hypocrisy, and impatience of our lives . . . our

self-indulgent appetites and ways, and our exploitation of other people . . . our anger . . . our envy . . . our dishonesty, negligence in prayer and worship . . . our false judgments . . . our prejudice and contempt . . . our blindness to human need and suffering, and our indifference to injustice and cruelty . . . we confess to you, Lord.[4]

Every Sunday in Lent, we read the Ten Commandments as well as Jesus' summary of the Law and the Prophets: "Love the Lord your God with all your heart and with all your soul and with all your mind and with all your strength. . . . Love your neighbor as yourself. There is no other commandment greater than these" (Mark 12:30–31). In this way, the liturgy holds up God's law as a mirror to help us see the specific ways in which we have not kept it. Countercultural though it may be, our liturgy exposes our wickedness, sin, and failure to love God and neighbor.

Sin is identified through Lenten preaching. Lent affords us six Sundays, plus a few special services—Ash Wednesday, Maundy Thursday, and Good Friday—to address sin and its cure. Like the hearers in Acts 2:37, we need to be "cut to the heart" through the anointed preaching of God's Word in order to be provoked to repentance. One of our Lent sermon series in recent years was based on Jesus' letters to the seven churches in Asia Minor (Rev. 2–3), which contain stinging, restorative rebukes that still ring true today.

Sin is identified by the Holy Spirit. All of our liturgy, preaching, and pastoring needs to be infused by the Holy Spirit, who alone brings conviction of sin (John 16:8). We cannot manufacture God's activity, but every one of us can submit to it.

Every Lent we pray, "Come, Holy Spirit," asking God to make us responsive to His presence, which is always calling out to us. He can open our blind eyes to see our sin and soften our hearts to repent of it rather than hide.

All this came together in my life last year. At Immanuel, we were progressing through a sermon series called "Deliver Us," from the Gospel of Mark. The idea is that we often ask God to deliver us from the big problems of the world, such as corruption, division, and evil. God answers that prayer in part by revealing how deeply rooted all those vices are in our own hearts. In the words of Russian author and historian Aleksandr Solzhenitsyn, "The line dividing good and evil cuts through the heart of every human being."[5] One of the problems in the world that always bothered me was how judgmental people can be. The people in my life whom I've found most difficult to forgive were those who had criticized me. I loved to judge the judgers, to hate the haters. But during that Lent, the Holy Spirit, using my wife, spiritual director, and a close friend, helped me see how often I silently criticize myself. This inevitably leads to harsh judgment toward other people whom I considered arrogant or mean. I always thought my harshest critics were *out there*. And like a crazy twist at the end of a movie, I realized that the critic was me. I can still remember feeling disoriented and "cut to the heart," yet full of hope that change was possible.

How Sin Is Confessed

After I recognized this sinful pattern, I was ready to confess my sin. This began in my private prayer life in a form you might recognize: "Jesus, have mercy! You have allowed me to see this pattern of judgment, and I need Your grace to change." He certainly had mercy on me in that moment. My prayer shifted from "deliver me from all those critical people" to "deliver me and the people in my life from my own inner critic!"

Soon after, I gathered for worship with all the other sinners in my church. We heard Jesus' summary of the law: love God with all your heart, soul, mind and strength, and love your neighbor as yourself. Since we had all failed on both accounts, we got down on our knees together and prayed an ancient Lenten confession of the truth:

> Almighty God, Father of our Lord Jesus Christ, maker of all things, judge of all men: we acknowledge and lament our manifold sins and the wickedness we have grievously committed time after time, by thought, word and deed against your divine majesty. We have provoked most justly your righteous anger and your indignation against us. We earnestly repent, and are heartily sorry for these our wrongdoings; the memory of them grieves us, the burden of them is too great for us to bear. Have mercy upon us, have mercy upon us, most merciful Father. For your Son our Lord Jesus Christ's sake, forgive us all that is past; and grant that from this time forward we may always serve and please you in newness of life, to the honor and glory of your name; through Jesus Christ our Lord. Amen.[6]

It's fitting for all who are bound together in Christ to be bound together in confession. None of us are free-floating individuals, but are living members of Christ's body (1 Cor. 12).[7] All of us that day heard the pronouncement of the gospel: Christ

Jesus has put away all our sins and given us His Spirit to empower us to love God and neighbor. I confessed my sin personally and liturgically, but there was more confession ahead for me.

I met with another pastor in my local network whom I respect so I could make a personal confession. Perhaps you are uncomfortable with the idea of confessing to a pastor, priest, or fellow Christian. If so, consider James 5:16: "Therefore, confess your sins to one another and pray for one another, that you may be healed." Jesus is our sinless and compassionate High Priest who forgives. But you and I need mature ambassadors of Christ (2 Cor. 5:20) who can hear our confession, pray for us, and proclaim the gospel to us.

So I met privately with Pastor Stephen, and we walked together through a liturgy called "Reconciliation of a Penitent." (You will find more specifics about this in chapter 11, where I explain in greater detail the process of personal confession.) As we began, he prayed for me: "The Lord be in your heart and upon your lips that you may truly and humbly confess your sins."[8]

I will never forget the question he asked me after I confessed my pattern of biting criticism. Without a trace of judgment, he asked, "Has this pattern damaged any of your relationships? Can you think of anyone that you've hurt?" Immediately, I envisioned a dear friend that I had unfairly and harshly criticized several months before.

A Season for Healing

Sin is not a static, private, one-dimensional event. It operates like a hurricane, wreaking destruction that is deep, wide, high, and long. It damages our relationship with God, with ourselves, with our community, and with the world. We can move with it and yield to its destructive power, or we can get on our knees and experience Jesus' healing power. Repentance is the Spirit-driven process that repairs the damage, one gospel conversation at a time. With each confession I made, I experienced how the love of Christ could restore each dimension of my life that sin had ruptured.

The final confession was face-to-face with my friend whom I had hurt. We reconciled in a tearful, honest conversation over Mexican food. I asked him how my words had impacted him, his relationships, and his life. Tempting though it was to skip all that with a quick "I'm sorry," the healing process required that I listen. We need to hear and reflect back upon the truth, of what we've done to destroy, and what Jesus has done to heal.

Repenting on Good Friday

New York City pastor Tim Keller sums up the gospel this way: "We are more sinful and flawed in ourselves than we ever dared believe, yet *at the very same time* we are more loved and accepted in Jesus Christ than we ever dared hope."[9] When we confess our sin and receive forgiveness, we experience both sides of the gospel. The light of Christ reveals our brokenness and belovedness at the same time, healing us in the process.

The "Bright Sadness" of the gospel operates all year round. During Lent, we intentionally turn our faces toward it, getting as close as we can to it. This journey culminates in the Good Friday service, when we remember and participate in the love of God in the cross of Christ. The liturgy of Good Friday shines the light of the gospel:

O God of unchangeable power and eternal light:
look favorably on your whole church, that wonderful
and sacred mystery; by the effectual working of your
providence, carry out in tranquility the plan of salvation;
let the whole world see and know that things which
were cast down are being raised up, and things which
had grown old are being made new, and that all things
are being brought to their perfection by him through
him all things were made, your Son Jesus Christ our
Lord; who lives and reigns with you, in the unity of the
Holy Spirit, one God, forever and ever. Amen.[10]

During the Good Friday service at Immanuel, we lay a large wooden cross on the floor. We place it in such a way that people can touch it as they kneel and pray. Everyone is invited to pray at the cross, taking as much time as they need to bask in Jesus' forgiving love. This is a tender moment. Not only do people touch the cross, but many wet it with their tears of lament and relief. Kneeling there, we are able to experience the beautiful exchange symbolized in the cross: Jesus takes our sin, and then He fills us with His love. He has "forgiven us all our trespasses, by canceling the record of debt that stood against us with its legal demands. This he set aside, nailing it to the cross" (Col. 2:13–14).

As we kneel and pray, we sing,

We glory in your cross, O Lord,
and praise and glorify your holy resurrection;
for by virtue of your cross
joy has come to the whole world.[11]

Prayer ministers are stationed throughout the sanctuary.

They are trained to hear confessions, declare the gospel, and intercede for anyone who comes forward. My leaders and I have seen Jesus heal the damage of sin every year. The grace of His cross is ministered to anyone ready to receive it. The relief is palpable as people divulge hard secrets, reconcile with God and neighbors, and praise Jesus for His redeeming grace. People are tasting heaven. There is no shortage of hope on Good Friday.

As the apostle Peter said, "He himself bore our sins in his body on the tree, that we might die to sin and live to righteousness. By his wounds you have been healed" (1 Peter 2:24). Jesus bore all our inherited sins, chosen sins, and collective sins. But instead of confessing them and asking for Jesus to take them away forever, we *instinctively* throw a tarp over them and pretend they don't exist. On Good Friday, and in all of Lent for that matter, we can hand over all our trash to Jesus. He set us free by taking every bag of refuse and dumping it onto the heap of hell. And He's still doing that today.

CHAPTER 6

Learning to Love the Future

Maybe your Easter service is held at sunrise at the beach, where new Christians shout their testimonies from the water before being submerged in the name of God the Father, Son, and Holy Spirit. Or perhaps you brew several pots of coffee and squeeze in every last folding chair in the living room that hosts your house church. It could be that you gather at midnight in a cathedral to welcome Easter with incense, choirs, and bells. Or you might wear your best hats and hang your best banners and sing your best songs in an old beloved church that your grandfather helped build. Or maybe your church plant livens up an urban school with vibrant liturgy and an engaging talk that connects with your skeptical neighbors. However your church celebrates Easter, I want to encourage you to be there. Without Lent, Easter tends to catch us off guard. But after the forty-day pilgrimage in the wilderness, we are ready to keep the Easter feast, to exult with all our heart that Jesus is alive.

Inasmuch as Lent has been preparing us pilgrims for Easter, Easter has a way of preparing us for heaven. It does so by satisfying our hunger, strengthening our commitment, and restoring our soul. In short, Easter—including the "little Easters" of Sunday worship throughout the year—is a taste of heaven, made available now through the power of the Holy Spirit. The kingdom of God is here. Come and see!

Satisfied Hunger

When a friend invites you over for dinner, the first way to compliment them is to come hungry. Hunger involves a kind of pain. Your stomach might rumble; your head might ache. Saying no to salty snacks and sweet treats all afternoon might wear you down. Do you keep delaying your gratification until dinner? That depends on whether you trust your friend to cook something good.

If you sneak a PB&J before heading out the door, arrive fashionably late, and pick at your food, you likely did not trust the host to satisfy you at their table. You assumed dinner would be bland, meager, or both. What an insult to the host! But if you showed up at their door truly hungry, pining for dinner to start, going back for seconds and thirds until you're stuffed—and in some cultures belching out your satisfaction—you have truly honored your friend. You came hungry and you let them satisfy you. In all likelihood, it will not be the last time you sit at that table.

Jesus has given us an open invitation to come to His house and be satisfied on Easter Sunday and beyond. That is why He referred to Himself as the Bread of Life who satisfies our hunger and the Living Water who satisfies our thirst (John 6:22–58; 7:37–39). His invitation reminds me of Isaiah's call to "Come, buy wine and milk without money and without price" (Isa. 55:1). Those who embrace the forty-day journey of Lent have done so because they trust Jesus is telling the truth about Himself: He is a feast for hungry people. And He was telling the truth about us: we are hungrier than we know.

Why do you spend your money for that which is not
bread, and your labor for that which does not satisfy?
Listen diligently to me, and eat what is good, and
delight yourselves in rich food. (Isa. 55:2)

Everyone who drinks of this water will be thirsty again,
but whoever drinks of the water that I will give him
will never be thirsty again. (John 4:13–14)

To the one who conquers I will grant to eat of the tree
of life, which is in the paradise of God. (Rev. 2:7)

And so we trekked out to the wilderness of Lent, unsatisfied
on purpose, clinging to the promise of something better than
the world could ever offer. So we put one weary foot in front of
the other, fueled by the hope of Easter. And one glad morning
we find that the journey is over. Lent has come to an end.

O God, you led your ancient people by a pillar of cloud
by day and a pillar of fire by night: Grant that we, who
serve you now on earth, may come to the joy of that
heavenly Jerusalem, where all tears are wiped away and
where your saints forever sing your praise; through
Jesus Christ our Lord.[1]

When we come hungry to Easter, Jesus is ready to satisfy
us with a heavenly meal. The fast is over, and dinner is served.
We are nourished by Jesus as Scripture is read, as the gospel
is preached, as songs are played, and as communion is served.
And the feasting continues in our dining rooms well after the
service is over.

Strengthened Commitments

Easter Sunday not only prepares us for heaven by satisfying our appetites, it also strengthens our commitment to the heavenly community. And let's be honest: our commitment to heaven can wane. This is why Jesus rebuked the church in Thyatira for her compromise and then promised, "The one who conquers and who keeps my works until the end, to him I will give authority over the nations" (Rev. 2:26). Temptation and suffering can compromise our allegiance to the King and His kingdom. This is one reason we show up on Easter: we need the living Christ to rule our rebellious hearts.

I experienced this in a tangible way during my first Easter Vigil put on by Church of the Resurrection. Easter Vigil began in the second century as one of the first ways to celebrate Jesus' resurrection, and many churches continue the tradition today. Laura and I had been attending Resurrection for one year, a year that had been a tough season for me. I was submerged in the rigors of my biblical exegesis master's program and was breathing the thin air of academia, where, even under godly professors at a Christian institution, a living faith can gasp for breath. Behind the Hebrew word analyses and the Greek sentence diagrams lay my inclination to sneer at Christian piety, and I modeled the Enlightenment posture of standing over the Scriptures with a microscope and a scalpel.

When Lent came around that year, I was half-convinced it was a good idea. I cannot fully recall my chosen discipline, but I likely chose a weak sauce fast from chocolate. I was more wrapped up in the tasks that would earn me better grades and recognition among my peers and professors. When I showed up to Vigil, I felt like I was trapped in a thick astronaut suit of doubt. As a result, I was unable to finish my first Lent with any sense of hope and joy, and I was plagued by a discouraging thought: *This is all a myth. This isn't true. I'm not supposed to celebrate.*

Laura and I had signed on to be received as members of the church at Vigil. So in the middle of the service we stood at the font next to the baptismal candidates and renewed our vows, renouncing Satan and pledging ourselves to Jesus. (The liturgy makes it possible for all Christians to renew their baptismal vows.) There was a special significance for those of us who were becoming members or getting baptized: we wore white robes over our clothes, which symbolize the white robes worn by the multiethnic assembly in heaven (Rev. 6:11; 19:1–8) and harken back to the catechumens who completed their Lenten training and wore white on the night of their baptism.[2]

I was not fully aware of the significance of ending Lent with a public confession of faith. From the earliest days of the church, baptismal vows were understood as an open declaration of war on Satan and his tyrannical rule. Showing up for baptism on Easter Eve was akin to showing up for your martyrdom.[3] Seen in this light, all of the Lenten disciplines were a "sacred fitness program" designed to prepare the body and soul for spiritual battle and victory that would follow your baptism.[4]

One stirring example of this pattern was Perpetua, a twenty-two-year-old wife and mother living in North Africa around AD 200. After becoming a catechumen, she was placed under house arrest where she was pressured by her father and the local magistrate to recant her beliefs. And why wouldn't she? Perpetua was a mother to a nursing infant and enjoyed the privileges of a well-to-do family in the Roman province of Carthage. Why not keep her Christian faith private, skip the baptism, and live in peace as a young wife and mother?

Perpetua was resolute. She stood for baptism at the risk of her own imprisonment, separation from her infant, and eventual martyrdom, holding fast under pressure from her father: "I can't be called by anything other than what I am: a Christian."[5] Soon after her baptism, she was taken from her home, separated from her baby, and thrown into an overcrowded jail. In her prison journal, Perpetua recounted nighttime visions of heavenly victory as she crushed the heads of creatures resembling Satan. These dreams, along with the leadership of her pastor, Sartus, and the encouragement from her fellow Christians, gave her ballast to receive a "second baptism" of martyrdom (Mark 10:38–39).[6] Perpetua and her maidservant, Felicity, were mauled by wild beasts and pierced by a sword in front of thirty thousand spectators.

Christians in Syria, Iraq, North Korea, and the Horn of Africa today face similar threats.[7] Like Perpetua they are pressured by their families, local authorities, and extremist militia groups to deny Christ and to resist the rite of baptism. Yet, like Perpetua, they are resolute and full of grace toward their persecutors. Showing up for their baptism is nothing less than showing up for their martyrdom—and victory. The world is watching.[8]

But what about for me and other Christians in the West? For us, baptismal vows might feel benign. But the battle is just as real. As we take or renew our vows, we are forsaking our lives to gain Christ. While we may not experience the "red martyrdom" of death, we can willingly embrace the "white martyrdom" of whole-hearted discipleship and witness (Rom. 12:1–2).[9] Unlike

Perpetua, many of us will live to fulfill an earthly vocation and raise our children to love and serve the Lord. But like Perpetua, in Christ we are dead to any of heaven's rivals and alive to the dominion of God (Rom. 6:1–11).

Whereas Lent is our annual training, renewing our baptismal vows on Easter is our annual reenlistment in the heavenly community. No matter how your home church structures the Easter service, your presence there is a pledge of your allegiance. The entire process of Lent and Easter strengthens our commitment to serve and rule in the kingdom as God always intended. The whole of our lives—appetites, loves, commitments, and habits—is set in order as we take our place as kings and queens under the reign of God. After all, we are not slaves anymore, but sons and daughters to be revealed in glory (Rom. 8:12–25). We are not minions pushed around by the powers of the age, but noble citizens of the city to come (Heb. 11:14–16). We hold court with angels and archangels, who with the glorified martyrs cheer our faithful passage through the suffering of this age (Heb. 12:1–2, 18–23). In the process we seek the welfare and flourishing of the city in which we live. And together we will witness God's kingdom come on earth as it is in heaven. Not only does Jesus satisfy us on Easter; He strengthens our commitment to the kingdom of God.

Restored Souls

So there I was, with a white robe on my body but a dark cloud over my heart, having just renewed vows I scarcely believed. I felt like a failure, a doubter, an onlooker—not exactly a candidate for martyrdom of any sort! Have you ever showed up for

Easter, or to any church service, feeling like that?

"He restores my soul." That simple promise of Psalm 23 is fulfilled in Jesus' resurrection and made present to us through His Spirit (Rom. 8:9–17). When we show up for Easter, we are setting our hopes on His power to restore what has died or become disconnected inside us. Others may have moved on to a quicker fix, but not us. We come broken and mortal, in need of the love of God in Christ. If He has not risen from the dead, we of all people are to be pitied most.

Though our souls are not fully restored in this life, the miracle of the resurrection is at work now. It is available to everyone, and when we show up on Sundays with our doubting, needy selves, there's no telling what God will do.

I will never forget how the Lord restored my soul the night I had made my vows. Eirik Olsen, a pastor to whom I had made confession that year, came to pray for Laura and me and anoint us with oil. He laid one hand on my forehead and another on my shoulder as he paused, listening to God.

The next moment caught me totally off guard. He prayed, "Lord, confirm in Aaron the vows he has made, and give him freedom from doubt." Speaking to me with the gentle strength of a spiritual father, he interrupted his prayer with a direct encouragement: "Aaron, I don't know whether doubt is something you're dealing with right now, but I'm praying for the Lord to deliver you."

I had not previously spoken to Eirik about doubt. As one who listened to God, he was simply able to name the spiritual chain holding me back from the joy of Easter. As soon as he interceded for me, the dark cloud lifted, the astronaut suit came off, and I was surprised by joy. I felt that I had been given spiritual breath and a desire to worship Jesus for the rest of the night. Thanks to the faithful prayer of a godly pastor, I experienced the renewing work of the Holy Spirit. It was like a down payment of Jesus' resurrection.

Barely a few minutes had passed after the vows when Stewart Ruch, the senior pastor who was leading the service, emerged to the front of the sanctuary with a full-throated announcement: "Alleluia! Christ is risen!"

The congregation roared back, "The Lord is risen indeed! Alleluia!"

Now it was time to celebrate! Bells rang, children danced in the aisles, and we made more noise than a packed home-team stadium that just won their first championship. Well, almost. It was the best kind of loud.

When Jesus Christ satisfies our hunger, renews our commitment, and restores our soul, we are ready to join the chorus of heaven in worship:

> Hallelujah!
> For the Lord our God
>   the Almighty reigns.
> Let us rejoice and exult
>   and give him the glory,
> for the marriage of the Lamb has come,
>   and his Bride has made herself ready;
> it was granted her to clothe herself
>   with fine linen, bright and pure. (Rev. 19:6–8)

On Easter Sunday, in every gospel-proclaiming church around the world, the visible church takes on the perspective and song of the invisible church. We are called to feast and sing and overflow with joy in the name of our risen Savior. In His great power and mercy, Jesus has fulfilled all our hopes, defeated our enemy, revived our dead hearts, brought true justice to the earth, and made all things new.

I was a beginner at Lent, capping a period of tepid fasting with feebly spoken vows. I had major discipleship work in the years that followed—and still do. My doubts and personal idolatries had marred the image of God. So much was—and is—unfinished in me, yet I tasted Jesus' resurrection power that night, and every Vigil and Eastertide since. Jesus restored my face so that I could behold His (2 Cor. 4:1–6). He helped me become who He intended me to be, and by doing so, He taught me "to love the future."[10]

CHAPTER 7

Answering Common Objections

In the previous chapters, we discovered the beauty and bene-fits of Lent. But maybe you still have your doubts. You might not be quite sold on the idea because you have some lingering qualms and questions that you feel haven't been fully satisfied. Let me address some of the common objections to observing Lent so that you may consider the season afresh.

Lent Isn't in the Bible

The word *Lent* is an old Saxon word meaning "spring," and no, it is not in the Bible. However, the path of Lent—prayer, fasting, and generosity over a period of time—is heavily emphasized by the authors of and characters in the Bible, including Jesus. The Bible commends a lifestyle of worship and devotion that looks considerably like Lent. Therefore, while the *word* is absent in the Bible, the *reality* of Lent is woven throughout the whole of Scripture, as we have discovered.

The Bible is replete with specific times set aside for devo-tion to God, including ones that last forty days. Moses fasted for forty days when he communed with the Lord on Mount Sinai (Ex. 34:28), Elijah fasted for forty days on his journey to meet God at Horeb (1 Kings 19:8), and, of course, Jesus fasted for forty days in the desert to prepare for His public ministry (Matt. 4:1–11).

Jesus told His followers not to fast while He, the Bridegroom, was present, but that they should after He departed (Matt. 9:15). In Matthew 6:16–18, Jesus teaches that when we fast, we should not do so in the manner of the Pharisees. Notice He did not say *if* you fast, but *when* you fast, assuming His followers would keep this practice. If Jesus Himself practiced and advocated for fasting, why should His church refrain from the practice in anticipation of Easter? While *Lent* is not in the Bible, the practice of Lent is indeed biblical and Christ-centered.

Colossians 2 Forbids Ascetic Fasts

Christians who are skeptical about Lent often quote Colossians 2:16–23:

> Therefore *let no one pass judgment on you in questions of food and drink*, or with regard to a festival or a new moon or a Sabbath. These are a shadow of the things to come, but the substance belongs to Christ. Let no one disqualify you, *insisting on asceticism* and worship of angels, going on in detail about visions, puffed up without reason by his sensuous mind, and not holding fast to the Head, from whom the whole body, nourished and knit together through its joints and ligaments, grows with a growth that is from God. If with Christ you died to the elemental spirits of the world, why, as if you were still alive in the world, do you submit to

regulations—"*Do not handle, Do not taste, Do not touch*
(referring to things that all perish as they are used)—
according to human precepts and teachings? These have
indeed an appearance of wisdom in *promoting self-made
religion and asceticism and severity to the body*, but they
are of no value in stopping the indulgence of the flesh.
(emphasis added)

The argument often goes like this: Paul is teaching us that
any exhortations to refrain from food and drink are in themselves an expression of self-made religion opposed to Jesus
Christ. Some have gone so far as to suggest that such calls to
fast are demonic,[1] quoting 1 Timothy 4:1–3:

Now the Spirit expressly says that in later times some
will depart from the faith by devoting themselves to
deceitful spirits and *teachings of demons* . . . who forbid
marriage and *require abstinence from foods that God
created to be received with thanksgiving* by those who
believe and know the truth. (emphasis added)

But is Paul forbidding a season of fasting in these passages?
No, Paul is opposing popular heresies that pitted the spiritual
against the physical. One strand of heresy that gained influence
in Asia Minor—where Timothy and those in Colossae lived—
was a belief that the physical world was inherently wicked.[2]
God's creation, including the human body, is evil, and the path
to true freedom is to reject all the trappings of the embodied
life—like food, drink, and marriage. That is truly a demonic
teaching. Christ made *all* things (John 1:1–14) and upholds
them by the word of His power (Heb. 1:3).

Moreover, by assuming humanity in His incarnation, Christ has redeemed the embodied life and declared it good![3] Christ is reconciling heaven and earth through His incarnation and cross (Col. 1:20). This is why the apostle John told his readers to test the spirits by affirming the incarnation, that Christ came *in the flesh* (1 John 4:2–3). So by all means, let us keep the feast! Let us celebrate the King of kings, and, if He sees fit, get married, have sex with our spouse, and rear children in Jesus' name (1 Cor. 10:31).

Let us also keep the fast so that our appetites may be reordered, not destroyed. Fasting and celibacy carried out in the name of Jesus and the power of the Holy Spirit affirm the human body in the story of redemption. It recalibrates the human appetite. Fasting done to exalt the ego or destroy the flesh is based on the "elemental spirits of the world" (Col. 2:20) and should be rejected as anti-Christ.

Let us not forget that the apostle Paul, who wrote both texts quoted above, chose both celibacy (1 Cor. 7) and fasting (Acts 9:9) for the sake of Christ. Immediately after his conversion on the road to Damascus where he saw the Lord of glory, Paul fasted from both food and drink for three days as he prayed in preparation for his baptism (Acts 9:9–19). Who would be better able to distinguish works-righteousness from genuine formation in Christ than Paul, who was once a master Pharisee? Yet as a converted Christian and apostle, he linked discipline of the body to fitness of the soul. Not only that, he enjoined the believers in Corinth to join him in bodily discipline:

> Do you not know that in a race all the runners run, but only one receives the prize? *So run that you may obtain*

it. Every athlete exercises self-control in all things. They do it to receive a perishable wreath, but we an imperishable. So I do not run aimlessly; I do not box as one beating the air. *But I discipline my body and keep it under control, lest after preaching to others I myself should be disqualified.* (1 Cor. 9:24–27, emphasis added)

In short, Paul did not forbid what his Lord commended. When church leaders serving Jesus call their people to a Lenten fast, they are contending for the spiritual freedom of their congregation. When false teachers denying the incarnation call people to a fast, they enslave people with lies. It's unfair and irresponsible to lump together a call to Christ-centered prayer, fasting, and generosity with the gnostic fasts that were popular in first-century Asia Minor.

Lent Is a Form of Works-Righteousness

Works-righteousness is an attempt to earn merit with God through certain behaviors. The hunger-strike panel in chapter 3 depicts the spiritual oppression of this approach. Any spiritual practice can get corrupted into the legalism of earning merit before God, including Bible study, social justice, or tithing. All of these practices are good, but if they are done in attempts to earn what Christ has already given us, we've enslaved ourselves.

Works-righteousness is a yoke of slavery that leaves us either anxious or arrogant before God. Even the Sinner's Prayer, which is intended to be a free response to God's great mercy, has become for many a fear-driven ritual intended to earn God's salvation. Many Christians pray it over and again, hoping they have said the right words or meant them sincerely enough.

We want God and the people in our life to approve of us, and we want to feel good about ourselves. Apart from our union with Christ, we are proud and fearful people, bent toward trying to earn merit. Any good action, prayer, or vocation, therefore, can become works-righteousness. But that doesn't mean we cease praying, giving, fasting, or loving our neighbor.

In order to operate in God's grace rather than in works-righteousness, we must first recognize the awesome character of God, who is gracious and slow to anger. This is seen most clearly in Christ, who died to take away our sins and renew our world, even while we were still God's enemies (Eph. 2:1–10; Rom. 5:10). Second, we can ask Jesus to live His life through us and to give us assurance of God's fatherly love (Rom. 8:12–17). Whether we are fasting or feasting, suffering or rejoicing, laboring or resting, we operate in union with Christ who did all that. Yet we continually need the Spirit to awaken us to obedience. As Dallas Willard wrote, "Grace is not opposed to effort, but is opposed to *earning*."[4] The season of Lent is a participation in God's life, not an entrance fee to heaven. Our security comes from resting in God's free gift.

Lent Is a Roman Catholic Practice Unsuitable for Protestants

While Lent is practiced by Roman Catholic and Eastern Orthodox Christians, it does not originate with or belong exclusively to them. Lent is also observed by most historic Protestant denominations, because it is a mere Christian practice belonging to all who follow Jesus. The majority of Christians around the world and throughout history are, or were, observers of Lent.

Do you affirm the truths about Christ contained in the Nicene Creed, that Jesus is fully God and fully man, put forward by the Council of Nicaea in 325? I hope so. The Nicene Creed is a theological gift to all Christians because it helps us interpret, teach, and live out the Scriptures responsibly. The same council of pastor-theologians who developed the Nicene Creed also formalized the practice of Lent, as we discussed in chapter 2. Why, then, would you receive the theological gift of Nicaea but not the pastoral one? Both are mere Christian in character and belong to the whole church.

Lent Is Just a Fad

It is true that Lent is *trending* among evangelicals, but that is far different than it being *trendy*. When something trends, it gains traction and attention. When something is trendy, it usually lacks substance in its nature and is thus dispensable, like a gimmick.

The Western church is all too enthralled with trendiness and gimmicks. But Lent is no more a gimmick than gathering for worship is. Lent is no more a fad than expository preaching is. Fog machines are a gimmick, as are movie-based sermon series. As of the writing of this book, it's trendy to preach from an iPad while wearing skinny jeans. That trend will fade someday, but history indicates that Lent is here to stay.

But is Lent simply an artisanal spiritual practice for people attempting to craft a mystique? One prominent theologian has suggested that evangelicals who observe Ash Wednesday are guilty of a "certain carnality (which desires) to do something which simply looks cool and which has a certain ostentatious spirituality about it."[5] I'm not sure how he discerned the psychological subtleties motivating people to practice Ash Wednesday. Such an assumption about others' motives is simply uncharitable.

We are not called to cast sweeping, disdainful judgments about people who practice Lent (or not). Yes, some who practice Lent are obnoxious about it. But that is not a sound reason to write off the season. Let us make our decision based on the biblical, theological, and pastoral value of Lenten practices. This side of heaven, none of us have entirely pure motivations. But we can choose a pathway where the Holy Spirit can transform them.

Ashes Cannot Help Us Repent

Ashes in Scripture are an outward sign of inner repentance before God. The book of Esther depicts the people of God using ashes to mourn and call upon Him for help (4:3). Jonah 3 commends the Ninevites for repenting in ashes before God. In ashes, Daniel prayed for God's mercy (9:3). Even Jesus affirmed the use of ashes to repent (Matt. 11:21). What we do with our bodies matters. As we discovered in chapter 5, ashes remind us of our mortality, our sin, and our need for Jesus' redemption.

Lenten Practices Should Be Lifelong

Many people ask, "Why should I give up something for forty days that I wouldn't for the rest of the year?" Or, "Why limit fasting, prayer, and generosity to the forty days of Lent? If this path is good for Christians, why not make it the default, lifelong posture?"

In short, heightened devotion is fruitful for a season, but cannot be sustained indefinitely. The Christian calendar offers a sustainable rhythm of which Lent is a part, and the fasting of Lent gives way to the feasting of Easter. Fasting and feasting are interconnected disciplines that teach us to love the King and His coming kingdom. In Lent, we learn to confess our sins, practice self-denial, and take on the humility of Christ. In Easter, we learn to rejoice, exult, and feast in Christ's victory. As historian William Harmless explains, "In these two liturgical seasons Christians drank in, by turns, the 'not yet' and 'already' of New Testament eschatology."[6]

It's important to remember that the Christian liturgical calendar developed in part out of the rhythms of Jewish practice. The Old Testament indicates seasons of both heightened devotion and celebration, including Levitically led "Sabbaths, new moons, and feast days" (1 Chron. 23:31) and "seasons of joy and gladness and cheerful feasts" (Zech. 8:19). Fasting and feasting were part of the "architecture of time"[7] in which Jesus participated as an observant Jew.

Practicing this rhythm of devotion each year has a cumulative impact. Each time we latch ourselves to Christ during Lent, He ministers maturity and grace that impact the rest of our year. Many Christians choose to keep, or modify, their Lenten disciplines for the rest of the year, as they have established helpful routines.

Finally, all Christians are welcome to exercise the disciplines they learned in Lent at any time. In the same way that every Sunday is recognized as a "little Easter," many Christians celebrate every Friday as a "little Lent" by fasting in remembrance of Jesus' passion and death. Other churches invite their members to fast in January as a way to devote their year to God. Setting time aside for certain practices allows us to focus more intently on God and to develop godly habits.

My Personal Experience with Lent Was Damaging

This is a serious concern. Some Christians were raised in a family or church that observed Lent but did not explain the vision behind the season. They were expected to fast, pray, and give their money without understanding why. Now that they have the option, they choose not to observe Lent. And it feels liberating! If that is you, I want to speak to you as a pastor.

First, your pain is legitimate. It's healthy to feel loss and sadness in response to this deficit in discipleship. If you feel angry for being forced to do something you did not choose, it's healthy to acknowledge that. Whenever arbitrary rules override our will, we will feel controlled rather than liberated. Many evangelicals feel similarly toward "quiet times"—personal Bible study and prayer—that they were forced to do growing up. Without a personally compelling reason behind the discipline, it becomes a rule—and rules can breed resentment.

Second, it might be healthy to seek Jesus apart from the season of Lent. Take a season for healing when you can hear Jesus' invitation to you personally. He can restore the freedom for which your soul longs. Seek out the wisdom of life-giving pastors and fellow Christians flourishing in Christ. Realize that fasting, prayer, and generosity done rightly can bring freedom and joy. It is the spirit in which we approach these forty days that makes the difference between lifeless legalism and vibrant devotion.

Finally, consider practicing Lent differently than you did previously. If there are "old wineskins" from your early formation—disciplines, prayers, or patterns that trigger a sense of fear and control—leave those aside. Ask Jesus to give you "new wineskins" and a fresh vision for his work in your life during Lent.

In part 2, I outline a process for discerning this vision and the means to train for it.

If you love Jesus Christ, cherish His gospel and live under the teachings of the Bible, I commend Lent to you. It's a season of spiritual devotion with roots in Jewish worship, the teachings of Jesus, and the practices of the apostles and early church. The Reformation-era critique of Lent as it was observed in medieval Europe was much needed. The solution, however, is not to cast aside Lent entirely, but to reform our practices so that they align with Scripture. This season of repentance is a gift to all Christians and good medicine for the modern church.

PART 2

THE
PATH
OF
LENT

CHAPTER 8

The Mountain of Fasting

In part 1, I addressed *why* Lent should be observed. Now I want to address *how* we should practice Lent, beginning with the most difficult and rewarding part.

Fasting in Lent is like hiking up a rugged, beautiful mountain. The journey is both spiritual and physical, involving our whole selves—and we don't come back the same. The path is fraught with perils, and we need wisdom from people who have ventured ahead of us. Here are some tips, warnings, and, above all, encouragements as you journey up the mountain.

A Safe Starting Place: The Partial Fast

One feature of Lent that I appreciate is its scalability. Nearly everyone can find a path that is both challenging and sustainable for them. The partial fast—known as the Lenten fast—involves cutting out part of your diet such as sugar or desserts, alcohol, meat, caffeine, or dairy products. Like the Christians in the early church, some people choose to cut out most parts of their diet, eating only vegetables, grains, or dried food.[1] The Eastern Orthodox canons call their faithful to give up meat, fish, eggs, dairy, wine, and oil.[2] A partial fast limits or removes the food and/or drinks associated with feasting. I typically give up sugar and alcohol for my partial fast.

Provided you do not cut out essential nutrition, a partial fast is a safe yet challenging way to practice Lent. You're not skipping any meals, but you're cutting out the extras. If you're accustomed to satisfying your every craving, a partial fast helps you learn to control your appetites. Jesus meets you in this training, inviting you to call out to Him when you feel irritated, bored, or restless.

A Partial Fast from Petty Distractions

Modern Christians have found incredible spiritual benefit in expanding their partial fast beyond the physical appetite to abstaining from other trappings of modern life. Many of us have instant access to any kind of entertainment, information, or mental stimulation we desire, for little to no cost. When I read Jesus' words about "the cares of the world" that choke out the Word of God (Matt. 13:22), I'm reminded of the glowing, chirping screen in my pocket. Its broadcasts can use up the bandwidth I need to meditate upon and share the good news.

Whatever might capture our imaginations and mental energy is fair game to give up for Lent: movies, TV, the news, social media, video games, sports, texting—you name it. Christ might ask us to lay one or more of these distractions aside for something better. Last year in the middle of Lent, a spiritual leader I respect asked a question during her teaching on the spiritual life: "What is Jesus asking of you?" A few moments after pondering that question, the answer for me was clear: streaming TV shows. I had been waiting several months to watch a show that was releasing that week, so it was tough to say yes to Him. Precisely because of the difficulty, I found that fast to be liberating. That show somehow had a hold on me, and Jesus gave me the prompting and the power to say no to it.

Discerning Your Partial Fast

Before I address how to discern your partial fast, let me offer two important caveats.

A partial fast is distinct from repentance of sin. Do not take a partial fast from using pornography or sleeping with your significant other. Rather, confess your sin to God, receive Christ's forgiveness, and take drastic, intentional steps to remove it permanently from your life. The same is true for any other sin, such as gluttony, racism, violent behavior, slander, envy, or deceit. A partial fast may help you repent of sin, but it is a different path altogether.

A partial fast is not an addiction treatment program. If you feel powerless to break a dependence on alcohol, sexual activity, gambling, drugs, overeating, or any other vice, seek professional help from a licensed counselor and an addiction recovery program in your church or community. Also seek support from your local pastor and church family. There is hope! The spiritual benefits of observing Lent with the people of God will be a support and encouragement as you walk the road of recovery.

With that said, here are a few questions to help you discern your partial fast:

- What cravings have a hold on me?[3]
- What would be truly liberating to leave behind?
- Short of an addiction, have I become dependent on a

particular food, drink, substance, or activity?
- What would be truly challenging to give up for Lent?
- What is Jesus asking of me?

After praying over these questions, I encourage you to select at least one luxury food or drink and at least one "modern distraction" to give up. If this is your first time observing Lent, keep it simple and make a short list of one or two abstentions that will challenge you without crushing you. Consider getting input from a mentor or pastor to ensure you set realistic goals. If you have already practiced the partial fast and are ready for more, then consider adding other items to your list.

If you have medical problems and diet restrictions that prohibit you from fasting from food, you are still welcome to participate in the spirit and discipline of Lent. It may require some creative experimenting. Please consult with your doctor, pastor, and others who can help you discern your Lenten path. You are not left out but are blazing a trail for others who share similar limitations.

The Next Challenge: The Whole Fast

The next stage of the hike is a steeper climb: the whole fast. This is not fasting from all food for all of Lent, but rather the practice of skipping entire meals for a short period of time—whether you go several hours, a full day, or several days without eating.

Those practicing this fast continue to drink water, juice, or other non-substantial liquids.[4] Drinking water keeps you hydrated. Juice can keep your blood sugar level stable, which keeps you focused. For juices, I recommend nonacidic options such as apple, grape, or those made at home from fresh fruit. I have also found that chicken broth helps sustain me.

Not everyone is called to practice the whole fast: small children, the elderly, pregnant or nursing mothers, people with prohibitive medical conditions such as diabetes, and those with a recent history of eating disorders such as anorexia nervosa or bulimia. If you have any concerns about fasting, please seek medical counsel from your doctor or a licensed medical professional before you begin. And do not practice the whole fast to improve your health or slim your waistline. This is not the reason for Lenten fasting.

Those who decide to make the trek of the whole fast will benefit from walking this road with others, preferably someone from your church, small group, or community. Even if they are not fasting with you, they can help you process the experience and pray for the Lord to strengthen you. If you are a pastor, fast with another pastor you trust. While it's true that Jesus warned us against broadcasting our fasting practices in public (Matt. 6:16–18), He was not forbidding the encouragement of a fellow pilgrim.

Options for the Whole Fast

If you are new to the whole fast, start by skipping breakfast or lunch once a week. Use that mealtime to feast on the presence of Christ as you pray or meditate on Scripture. For the other meals that day, eat enough to sustain your energy but not enough to fully satisfy your hunger. This will give you a glimpse of the cost and reward of the whole fast.

The next step for the whole fast is going twenty-four hours without food once per week. Eat a light dinner the night before, get a good night's sleep, and then skip breakfast and lunch. You can break the fast at dinner the following night. When I practice this, I often call my wife, Laura, mid-afternoon to ask about our dinner plans!

If the Lord leads and if your body can sustain it, you may extend your fast to two to three days. I encourage you to save this fast for Holy Week to join the practice of the global and historic church. Again, keep yourself hydrated with water and juices or broths, and consult with a medical professional in advance if you have any concerns.

Whole Fasts in Christian History

Here are a few historic ways that you can practice the whole fast in Lent:

At the beginning of Lent: Ash Wednesday. Fasting on Ash Wednesday is a bedrock practice of the ancient church. It situates us into a posture of humility and need as we prepare to receive the ashes and journey with Christ in the forty days of Lent.

In the middle of Lent: Wednesdays and/or Fridays. To keep in step with ancient Christians, I recommend you practice your whole fast on Wednesdays to commemorate Jesus' betrayal, Fridays to remember His death, or both. Many Christians continue this practice throughout the year. Remember that just as every Sunday is a "little Easter," so every Friday can be a "little Lent."

At the end of Lent: Maundy Thursday through Easter. As we discovered in part 1, fasting in preparation for Easter—and for baptism—began soon after Christ's resurrection and ascension. This fast lasts about sixty hours from the Maundy Thursday evening service to the Easter service Sunday morning. In these hours, we remember Jesus' passion for the life of the world, and ask Him to make His love known to us and our world. If a sixty-hour fast seems too daunting, you can scale this back by fasting only on Good Friday. However, if you are preaching or leading services during this time, please do not fast (see survival tip number 6 below).

Let's make the climb of fasting together during Lent this year. It will involve our whole selves—spiritually, physically and emotionally. But it's wholly worthwhile.

Fasting Survival Tips

Since fasting in Lent may be new for many readers, let me offer seven survival tips for fasting. These are all built upon the experiences of others who have fasted in Lent and have learned wisdom along the way. We need their perspective so that we do not cave in to the temptation to be fatalistic ("I'll never make progress, I can't do it, I quit!"), perfectionistic ("I have to design the perfect Lent discipline and get the most out of it!"), or moralistic ("I'm killing it at Lent, and God loves me more as a result!"). We also need to be aware of the ways other pilgrims make the journey sustainable.

1. Celebrate the Feast Days

As I mentioned in chapter 2, every Sunday is a "little Easter" and is not included in the forty days of Lent. So feast in the name of Jesus on Sundays! This practice keeps your Lenten vows sustainable and allows you to celebrate Jesus' resurrection along the way to Easter.

2. Celebrate the Gospel

Friends, Christ has died! Christ is risen! Christ will come again! He created you, and when you turned from Him and fell into sin and death, He had compassion on you. He left heaven to give His very life for you, and He rose again in victory over sin and death. Even now He is making all things new by re-uniting heaven and earth, and His kingdom will have no end. You can live under His gracious rule now, wherever you are. When you turn to Jesus, He makes you God's adopted child, whose inheritance is a love that reaches beyond all depth, width, height, and length. When we practice Lent, we need to soak in these precious truths to avoid the trap of works-righteousness. Gospel truth is the feast that makes all our fasting possible.

3. Take the Long View

The daily experience of Lent can be boring or discouraging. We can expect discomfort, irritation, and doldrums. Given that Lent is like a "spiritual spring," the seeds we sow remain hidden for most of the season. Yet if we persevere, the fruit of God's deep work in us will eventually grow.

Karen, a friend and leader at Immanuel Anglican, decided one year to give up coffee for Lent. She describes the pain of losing a multisensory, comforting ritual she had come to love: "the smell, the taste, grinding the beans, the way the strong aroma fills my kitchen as my coffee pot sputters away, and the caffeine-buzz feeling in the morning." Karen was half-expecting that a spiritual high would replace the caffeine buzz, but it never did. "Two weeks into Lent, I was doing okay. I drank hot water and tea but missed the coffee. I hoped to feel some sort of spiritual growth in making this change. I had been taught that giving something up for Lent was a way to cultivate desire for Jesus. Every time I felt that desire for coffee pop into my head, I wanted to pray that I would want Jesus just as much as I wanted the coffee. But giving up coffee for Lent did not feel good, or even spiritual."

The harvest for Karen came much later than expected, and was more substantial than a spiritual high. "After Lent had ended I reflected upon the fact that fasting for Lent really wasn't about me feeling a certain way. But after the pain of discontent, it ended! Easter came, and I received incredible solace in knowing that I didn't have to deal with my longing forever. Lent was about Jesus and how He has changed our reality—my reality."

And like all of us who are learning to love the future, Karen still deals with the reality of unmet desires. But Lent taught her to take the long view. "Most days I'm okay, but other days these desires seem tremendously large. Life feels hard and I feel cranky. Even though I can't always feel it, I trust that the promises of the resurrection are real. So I pray and I wait and I believe that one day the reality of Easter will fill my heart and soul and mind and body fuller than I could ever imagine. I will be satisfied once and for all. And my heart will overflow with joy."

I admire Karen's honesty in describing the daily struggle of self-denial in following Jesus. We all are on a long journey. A day is coming when all our sufferings will be transformed into glory:

> For I consider that the sufferings of this present time are not worth comparing with the glory that is to be revealed to us . . . we ourselves, who have the firstfruits of the Spirit, groan inwardly as we wait eagerly for adoption as sons, the redemption of our bodies . . . if we hope for what we do not see, we wait for it with patience. (Rom. 8:18–25)

I find that when I am most tempted to give in to despair or self-indulgence, the encouragement of a fellow Lent pilgrim, who can remind me of the long view, gives me the strength I need to continue the journey.

4. Consider Others When Choosing Your Lenten Path

Before you make major decisions about how to practice Lent, consider the people in your life. Your chosen discipline(s) will also impact them. I know friends whose fast from coffee made them insufferable, and their spouses eventually put the kibosh on it! Loving God and others—the two greatest commandments—are interconnected, so give the significant people in your life a voice before you dive headlong into lifestyle changes.

5. Let Failure Teach You

Proverbs 24:16 says, "The righteous falls seven times and rises again." Failure is an unavoidable aspect of Lent. Depending on how you approach it, it either traps you or leads you to the next stage of growth. Alexander Schmemann put it like this:

> No progress in Christian life is possible, alas, without the bitter experience of failures. Too many people start fasting with enthusiasm and give up after the first failure . . . [when] the real test comes. If after having failed and surrendered to our appetites and passions we start all over again and do not give up no matter how many times we fail, sooner or later our fasting will bear its spiritual fruit.[5]

My friend Will was incredibly disciplined during his first Lent. But in the second year, "I just failed—miserably," he said. "I always forgot to fast on Fridays, went on social media anyway, I avoided the poor so I wouldn't have to give money that I pledged

I would. And I was feeling horrible about my faithlessness."

He processed his experience with a godly counselor, whom he half-expected would respond with judgment. "But then the counselor leaned in and told me that failure was integral to the whole process, and that when we fail in our promises, God is utterly faithful and victorious." Will's compassionate counselor ministered the gospel to him when he felt burdened and discouraged. "That has entirely changed the way in which I practice Lent," Will said. "It is a time to experience God's grace. It is a profound way to participate in the temptation and death of Christ, looking forward to His victorious resurrection over sin and death."

Without the Holy Spirit, failure can make us discouraged, self-hating, and cynical. This is not God's intention. Let your failures remind you of your need for Jesus and the community He has given you. Let them display God's power in your weakness. Only then will you have the capacity to endure till Easter.

Schmemann further explains,

> Between holiness and disenchanted cynicism lies the great and divine virtue of patience—patience first of all with ourselves. There is no shortcut to holiness. . . . There is no fast without challenging our capacity, without introducing into our life a divine proof that things impossible with men are possible with God.[6]

6. Do Not Fast on Days When You Are Preaching or Leading a Service

Spiritual leadership expends tremendous amounts of energy. If you're a church leader, please eat on days when you're leading a service, preaching, or doing intensive pastoral care. This is especially important if you are conducting Holy Week services. You need to sustain your energy, so fast on different days. I have colleagues who have nearly fainted while leading a Holy Week service on an empty stomach.

7. Fear Spiritual Numbness More Than Physical Discomfort

I don't enjoy the discomforts of Lent, and neither does my friend Josh. But both of us have found that hunger pains wake us up spiritually. Josh admits that until this last year, he has managed to practice Lent while avoiding physical discomfort: "I have never given up anything costly or important to me. And I have attempted to pass through Lent on my own power."

Unsurprisingly, Josh has always felt underwhelmed on Easter Sunday: "After all, other than salvation, what does He have to offer that I don't already have?" Josh was always physically satisfied, and this left him spiritually numb. He told me that he'd been inclined to immediately gratify whatever desire he had—for food, drink, convenience, or just some peace and quiet from his kids.

Yet the Holy Spirit used a Lenten sermon from Jesus' rebuke to the church in Laodicea (Rev. 3) to awaken Josh to the perils of self-satisfaction. "I realized that ceaseless physical comfort made me spiritually numb," Josh said. "My attitude toward Christ's redeeming work mirrored that of the Laodiceans: 'I am rich, I have prospered, and I need nothing'" (Rev. 3:17).

That night was a turning point for Josh, freeing him to embrace the pain of discomfort for the greater reward of dependence on his Savior. Josh now looks forward to the seasons of self-denial because he's learned that the costly, uncomfortable disciplines of Lent create a spiritual poverty that sweetens and enriches his communion with God. Like Josh, I naturally fear physical discomfort. Yet spiritual numbness is far worse. I don't want to miss out on the experience of being weak and dependent and thus spiritually alive in Christ.

CHAPTER 9

The Valley of Prayer

Eight years ago, Laura and I faced a crisis in our marriage. Following God's call, we moved from Chicago to Washington, D.C., with our sons. Gus was two years old, and Sam was one week old. That's right, Laura gave birth just seven days before we moved. We were in a new city, and I had no job.

I remember coming home for dinner. I would look at Laura, and she would glance at me. While I was job hunting in humid July, she spent her days in a new, rented house, caring for a newborn and a toddler. Weeks after the move, I still didn't have a job, and we were exhausted. In those moments, neither of us batted our eyelashes or even smiled. Beneath our grimaces and irritation was an ocean of tears, grief for what was behind us and anxiety about all that lay ahead. We took turns crying that summer. It was undoubtedly a crisis, but somehow we'd never been closer.

Communion and Crisis

The paradox of Lent is that it creates a spiritual crisis that leads to stronger communion with God and others. This is the "Bright Sadness" that animates our prayers, even if only in the form of tears or groans or old psalms. In Lent, we are vexed by our weakness, feel like aliens in a strange land, and know all too well that it is not good for us to be alone.

As we prepare for Easter, we need new prayer habits to help us confront our isolation, pain, and temptations. As a result, we come to the end of ourselves in the best way possible. This process trains us to cling to Jesus and His church rather than using either as a quick fix for a better life.

When Jesus was praying in the garden of Gethsemane in preparation for the cross, He called His disciples to keep watch with Him rather than withdrawing to sleep (Matt. 26:36–46). Jesus knew that the crisis of His impending death was meant to draw Him into deeper communion with His Father, and He implored His disciples to stay awake with Him, to join Him in that crisis-filled communion. When we pray in Lent, it's almost as if we are hearing that invitation for ourselves: "Watch and pray that you may not enter into temptation. The spirit indeed is willing, but the flesh is weak" (Matt. 26:41).

So instead of escaping the heat of crisis and doing what we want, we stay put and keep watch. We grasp hands with Jesus and our fellow Christians and ask the Father to deliver us from evil. By the time we reach Easter morning, our hope in Jesus' resurrection is richly rewarded with joy and thanksgiving. Let's consider three ways Christians throughout history have "kept watch" during Lent.

Praying in Community

So how should we pray in Lent? For starters, we go to church. We prioritize being present every Sunday possible, singing heartily in worship, engaging in the prayers, confessing our sins and our faith, listening receptively to the reading of Scripture and to the sermon, and partaking in the communion meal. Whether your church gathering is liturgical or not, church attendance is vital to a healthy prayer life. Your leaders work hard to prepare a service that will connect you deeply with God and His people. So drink deeply from that spiritual fountain on the Sabbath. Draw enough water to hydrate you for the rest of the week.

But you're not at church only to receive and consume. Your presence and prayers might seem weak to you, but they strengthen everyone else. When we show up to the weekly assembly of saints, we stir up the faith of our fellow pilgrims in Lent. Our prayers strengthen theirs, and theirs ours. The author of Hebrews—a pastor, no doubt—called the flock to draw near to God "with a true heart in full assurance of faith" and added that they should "consider how to stir up one another to love and good works, not neglecting to meet together, as is the habit of some, but encouraging one another, and all the more as you see the Day drawing near" (Heb. 10:22–25).

Praying in community continues after we have scattered from our Sunday gathering. Christians around the world mark the days of Lent through morning and evening prayers, which include confession, praise, petition, and daily readings from the Scriptures. I love to pray the Psalms in Lent, especially those that help me lament and express sorrow over my sin and the brokenness around me. How you use common prayer—joining in with the saints worldwide—is up to you. There's no mandate, only an invitation. The point is that you're not alone in praying. You need the saints, and they need you.

If your church offers a small-groups ministry, join one during Lent. If your pastor asks you to lead a small group, consider saying yes. Lean in and participate when it's time to pray.

Anglicans have a liturgy, and set readings, for morning and evening prayer, found in the *Book of Common Prayer*. This is a mere Christian way to pray together, so you do not have to be Anglican to use it. If you would like to learn how to pray with us, go to aarondamiani.com and click on the "Resources" tab. There you can download our liturgy and daily Scripture readings for free. The Morning and Evening Prayer liturgies include clear instructions for those who are leading or participating. Even if no one joins you in these morning or evening prayers, you are praying with Christians around the world.

Another simple way to pray with God's people is to pray a psalm in the morning, in the evening, or both. You can either choose the selected psalm from the daily readings, or choose your own. Some great psalms for Lent are 6, 22, 31, 32, 38, 51, 86, 102, 130, and 143.

Praying in Honesty

In America, we love upbeat songs and positive prayers. One journalist for the data-driven news outlet FiveThirtyEight recently studied the lyrics of contemporary Christian music and found that about 75 percent of the songs were "unremittingly positive."[1] Many of these songs reflect a well-meaning desire to communicate gospel hope. To be sure, expressing optimism and hope in a dark hour can reflect true courage and virtue, but not if cheeriness comes at the expense of truth. Sometimes positivity is nothing less than cover-up speech intended to silence grief and rage. In our culture, we often see a disconnect between the real trials of human experience and the sub-Christian instinct to use Jesus to cheer people up. While the complaints of a "Debbie Downer"[2] are unhelpful and wearying, stuffing our prayers and songs with happy talk is unrealistic, if not dangerous.

Genuine Christian hope stands strong, yet it can also suffer and give voice to suffering. Reflecting on the Psalms, biblical scholar Walter Brueggemann explains,

> When we pray and worship, we are not expected
> to censure or deny the deepness of our own human
> pilgrimage. Rather, we are expected to submit it openly
> and trustingly so that it can be brought to eloquent and
> passionate speech addressed to the Holy One.[3]

Let everything in human life be brought to speech, and let all speech be brought to God. Faithful prayers are, if nothing else, honest. And honesty evokes passion, whether in prayer with God or in conversation with a trusted friend. The season of Lent trains us to pray honestly, faithfully. The tone, liturgy, and theological focus of Lent provide a blast chamber of prayer, where our screams can find their way to the throne of grace. The Suffering Servant who wailed, "My God, my God, why have you forsaken me?" (Matt. 27:46) as He was executed by evil men can hear and handle our worst words.

Meredith worships at Church of the Resurrection in Washington, D.C. Her first experience of Lent began with lament. "In the weeks leading up to Lent," she said, "I found the spirit of the season sharpened when sorrow and suffering became my unexpected travel companions. A family member received diagnosis of an incurable disease, a romantic relationship ended abruptly, and a young sibling ran away from home, sparking a frantic thirty-six-hour search. When I arrived at the Ash

Wednesday service, my skin prickled with grief. The upcoming fast stretched out in front of me like the harsh and unforgiving tundra. I wept while my pastor made the sign of the cross in ashes on my forehead."

As she walked into the forty-day journey, Meredith was strangely consoled by the suffering described in the book of Job. "Few stories address the raw uncertainty of suffering like Job does," she said. "It is a place for questions, it is a place to grieve, and at forty-two chapters long, it is the perfect length for Lent. I followed Job's fall from prosperity and health to ashes and potshards, the seven days of silence, the stanzas of speech between Job and his comforters, the divine cross-examination."

Meredith's grief trained her in Christian hope, which leads to celebration. As she persevered through Holy Week with Easter in sight, she found her hopes altered and increased.

> I longed less for things I had given up and more for
> the coming of the One who transforms sorrow and
> suffering into grace and glory. Time wore on. I felt
> weary, raw, and ready. "Hold on a little longer," I told
> myself. "Easter is coming." Hoping for Easter nurtured
> my hope in the final celebration to come outside of
> time. . . . [On Easter] the music swells, the incense
> rises, and the drab banners of mourning drop, revealing
> a kaleidoscope of color and light. Afterward, there
> is a great feast, an abundance of wine and laughter
> into the early hours of Easter. We celebrate like the
> children at the end of C. S. Lewis's *The Last Battle*:
> "The term is over: the holidays have begun. . . . This is
> the morning."[4]

Our communities need Christian hope as much as ever. We live in an age of great suffering and division. Our social fabric is tearing. We are losing our capacity to stand together and grieve in solidarity. The parade of tragedies at home and abroad is numbing us. Here in Chicago, we feel powerless to stop violence that is consuming the lives of children and teens. My fellow Chicago pastor Ernest Gray just eulogized a twenty-four-year-old African American male who was gunned down in his West Side neighborhood. At the time, he was one of the 344 killed and the 2,071 shot in our city during the first half of 2016. As the bodies stack up, our emotional capacity goes down.

One of the gifts the local church can offer is to reconstitute broken relationships and heal divisions. No church does that perfectly, but it is our humble gift to the world to weep with those who weep (Rom. 12:15) and bear one another's burdens (Gal. 6:2). We can provide a sacred space for honest prayers and teach people the healing language of lament.

During your times of prayer this Lent, keep the following in mind:

If you experience emotions such as anger, fear, shame, or sadness, express those feelings to God. Remember, honesty evokes passion; this can deepen your prayer life. I find it helpful to hand-write in a journal with the heading "How I'm Honestly Doing Right Now." I take the filter off and put words to my pain, offering it as a prayer to God. You can then turn to Scripture and let it speak into your struggle.

If someone in your life shares a crisis with you, write it down on a prayer list. Keep the list handy so you can intercede for them throughout Lent.

Take note of the pain of your community, and be in prayer

where your community is suffering. If you're a pastor, lead your congregation in a time of corporate lament on their behalf.

Finally, remember that as we grieve the world we know, Jesus is preparing the world God wants.[5]

Praying in Weakness

The spiritual crisis of Lent teaches us to deny our seemingly respectable religious selves. As Jesus takes us into the wilderness, He teaches us to pray like children. And for most of us, this is often an arduous process.

It's not cool to be needy. We tend to avoid people with a desperate look in their eye, opting instead for those who seem to have their life in order. And so to keep up appearances, we cover our own neediness with the fig leaves of confidence and competence. "Work is intense, and I'm traveling again next month. But I love what I do!" "It's been a crazy busy year for our kids, between soccer and honor society." "We broke up, but he's a great guy. We both learned so much. I'm doing great, actually."

As these niceties sail through our whitened teeth, we grow lonelier. Behind the smile is our genuine human need for connection, provision, and assurance. Need opens the door to relationship and communion. If our lives are great and lovely, then who of us needs God or a neighbor?

Polite words can sustain a conversation, which is sometimes wise and necessary. But in the long run, covering up our desperation projects a false self, limiting our capacity to commune with God and others. Soul-refreshing conversations are honest and reveal joy and sorrow, strength and weakness. Desperation is the end of our pride and the beginning of our prayer life. This is why Jesus warned us that "unless you turn and become like children, you will never enter the kingdom of heaven" (Matt. 18:3). When we drop our pretenses and tell God what we need like a child, we discover an affectionate, responsive Father.

Educator and author Paul Miller has opened up the reality of prayer to thousands of Christians who feel like failures at it. Commenting on Jesus' words in Matthew 18:3, Miller writes,

> What do [children] ask for? Everything and anything. If they hear about Disneyland, they want to go there tomorrow. How often do little children ask? Repeatedly. Over and over again. They wear us out. Sometimes we give in just to shut them up. How do little children ask? Without guile. They just say what is on their minds. They have no awareness of what is appropriate or inappropriate.[6]

I find myself most responsive to my kids when they are calling out in desperation. When my son Sam injured himself after falling off his scooter, I heard him wailing, and I sprang into action. He didn't even say, "Dad!" He just cried loudly, and because he's my son, I went running in his direction.

In Lent, I find myself in Sam's position: failing, hurting, not okay. And so I have taken up the simplest prayer of all: "Jesus!" Sometimes that's all I can muster, yet it's always enough. Calling on the name of Jesus is shorthand for a prayer of the ancient church known as the "Jesus Prayer": "Jesus, Savior, Son of God, have mercy on me, a sinner!" This simple prayer is based on Jesus' parable of the Pharisee and the tax collector. Jesus tells the story of a Pharisee who approaches God on the basis of his high-functioning merit: "God, I thank you that I am not like other men, extortioners, unjust, adulterers, or even like this tax collector. I fast twice a week; I give tithes of all that I get" (Luke 18:11–12). You and I are not likely to use pompous words like that, but we are tempted to have the same attitude of comparison and self-sufficiency. In contrast, the tax collector is in touch with his desperation and gets right to the point: "God, be merciful to me, a sinner!" (Luke 18:13). Jesus goes on to tell us that the man who called on God in his need went home justified and exalted.

Praying the Jesus Prayer is not an empty formula or incantation, but a way of abiding with God in our state of desperation during Lent. The Jesus Prayer is not only ancient and widely used, but also honest, intimate, and personal. Whatever situation you find yourself in, you can improvise on the Jesus Prayer, especially during Lent: "Jesus Christ, Bread of Life, I'm hungry, grouchy, and have a headache. Feed me in this spiritual wilderness!" "Jesus, Servant of All, I'm consumed with my own needs. Give me strength to love and serve my coworkers!" "Jesus, Friend of Sinners, I feel lonely and sad. Be near to me!"

Prayers like this are what Eugene Peterson has called "First Language," the non-articulate babbling between an infant and parent.[7] We tend to complicate prayers with information and manipulation. But the Holy Spirit can help us recover the childlike simplicity of praying, "Abba! Father!" (Rom. 8:15)

As our self-sufficiency is chiseled away during Lent, we have an opportunity to draw near to God and His people as we pray, in honesty and in our weakness.

CHAPTER 10

The Adventure of Almsgiving

Several years ago, Laura and I met Reggie at a neighborhood barbecue. He and his wife were switching back and forth between socializing with neighbors and taking care of their six-year-old son, who was off by himself screaming about something. Reggie and I shared an interest in running, so we hit it off pretty easily. But he seemed stressed, and so did his wife. They left shortly thereafter, but not before we exchanged phone numbers.

Reggie and I went running the following week. As we found our pace, he apologized for the unusual behavior of his son, who has Asperger's Syndrome. Once we had run a few miles, Reggie dropped more heavy news: His wife was talking about separating. Caring for a special needs child brought them both incredible stress, and their marriage hung by a thread. And signs indicated that she was romantically involved with another man.

About six weeks later, his wife filed for divorce, leaving Reggie to care for his son. They were in a tough spot. In between legal fees and extra childcare expenses, Reggie's finances were maxed out, and he was exhausted. So we had them over for dinner a lot, let their son play with our kids after school, and occasionally prayed with him about his situation. Reggie was a lapsed Catholic.

We didn't solve his problems, but we let our lives remain

intertwined. Along the way, some of his family stress became ours. His son's behavior sometimes frightened and frustrated our kids, and on occasion Reggie asked too much from Laura and me. We had to learn to set boundaries without disconnecting from him. It was messy, as love usually is. But strangely enough, the whole experience of loving Reggie's family deepened our love for Jesus in a way that fasting and prayer alone never could. And in the process, we celebrated God's good provision for him and his son.

The last Lenten discipline is *almsgiving*, a quaint but charming word for "generosity." In my experience, almsgiving is an adventure. Generosity, as it is taught in Scripture and modeled by Jesus, is relational, not transactional. Although generosity in Lent sometimes involves cutting a check, this is never the heart of it. Biblical generosity is a posture of openness to bless our neighbor with our personal presence, our love, and, in some cases, our resources.

Generosity is perhaps the most complicated of all the Lenten disciplines because it connects us to people, and people are complicated. So are their situations. As we take risks to bless our neighbor in simple, Spirit-led ways, we are not guaranteed a return on investment. We are not in control of the outcome. It might feel like a waste since we are not even solving their problems. We are simply showing up to a relationship we might otherwise ignore and offering what we can to alleviate their suffering.

In books, sermons, and teachings on Lent, fasting seems to get the most attention and generosity the least. Many who practice Lent aren't even aware that generosity is a historic practice of the season. Generosity works in tandem with prayer and fasting to shape us into Christlikeness. And because of generosity, our fasting and prayer have a relational impact, turning us outward so that we do not overlook Christ in our neighbor. In this way, generosity marks our forty-day journey with a relational, loving quality. By the time Easter rolls around, our connection to God and neighbor is better aligned with God's vision for a flourishing life.

The Neighbor Fund

AJ and Nancy are leaders in our church who model Lenten generosity in an inspiring and sustainable way. On the side of their fridge they post an envelope labeled "Neighbor Fund." During Lent, AJ and Nancy stuff that envelope with cash from their personal spending allowance. When they would normally use those funds for modest luxuries, like buying a shirt at Target or ordering in Thai food on a Friday night, they squirrel it away and start praying for ways to love their neighbors financially.

In their experience, there's no telling in advance how the Neighbor Fund will get used between Ash Wednesday and Easter. But they are foodies, so their favorite way to spend it is by hosting neighbors for dinner, especially those who might not be able to reciprocate. Sometimes they find themselves buying food for their hungry neighbors in Chicago or taking a meal to a new mother. In one instance, the Neighbor Fund helped finance a college student's mission trip. AJ and Nancy scout out opportunities to throw a party or to make someone's day. They ask the Holy Spirit to lead them to a neighbor in need. They take joy in welcoming personal inconveniences so they can give generously. This is one of the ways that the love of God begins to *overflow* during the season of Lent.

A Well-Watered Garden

When Lenten generosity, prayer, and fasting are practiced together in a Spirit-led way, we become like a well-watered garden. Gardens that are properly irrigated bear fruit for others. Similarly, people who are irrigated by the Lord produce fruit that benefits the people around them. The poor and dispossessed can glean from the overflow of our time, energy, and resources, and experience God's grace in the process (Lev. 19:9–10).

Isaiah 58, a classic passage that connects fasting, prayer, and generosity, harps on this image of a well-watered garden. In this passage, God speaks through His prophet Isaiah to rebuke the people of Israel for their selfishness. They were fasting from food to appear religious and in the process became stingy, mean-spirited, and unjust in their dealings. They failed to connect the dots between being hungry for God and relieving the hunger of their neighbor. So the Lord gave them a vision for something better:

> If you pour yourself out for the hungry
>   and satisfy the desire of the afflicted,
> then shall your light rise in the darkness
>   and your gloom be as the noonday.
> And the Lord will guide you continually
>   and satisfy your desire in scorched places
>   and make your bones strong;
> and you shall be like a watered garden,
>   like a spring of water,
>   whose waters do not fail. (Isa. 58:10–11)

Most people I know would not describe themselves as a

well-watered garden with enough resources to spare. They feel limited in their capacity to give money, energy, and time. Perhaps they are still paying off loans, dealing with chronic fatigue, or working seventy hours a week. For this reason, talk of generosity and almsgiving can trigger guilt or defensiveness.

This is why I find Isaiah's imagery helpful. "You shall be like a watered garden" is a tender promise from a generous God, not a shakedown for resources we do not have. He is a good Father who is calling us to move from fear-based survival to a lifestyle of overflow for the life of the world. Commenting on this passage, Old Testament scholar John Oswalt unpacks the spiritual meaning of the garden imagery:

> The person who has the light of God in his or her life . . . whose soul is refreshed in the deserts of life and whose body is strengthened by him will be a *watered garden.* . . . That is, such a person will have a rich supply of gifts to share with others; they will be a source of delight and encouragement. They will not be like the thornbush in the desert, of all whose energy is consumed in the grim business of survival, but will have fruits and flowers to give from the overflow of their abundance. . . . Those who know the Lord, as shown by their treatment of the powerless, will never lack for the water of the Holy Spirit in their lives. They will have water for their own lives and more than enough to pour out on the afflicted souls around them.[1]

God takes good care of His people, feeding them spiritually and physically. And then He commissions them to take good care of the weak, spiritually and physically. This is not a zero-sum game of ham-fisted exchanges but a teeming and tender expression of heaven on earth. Yes, we are called to cultivate value and work hard in the process. But the margins of that value are reserved for the poor, the sojourner, and the weak. In this way, we reflect God's generosity to us in Christ, who became impoverished for our sake (2 Cor. 8:9).

So how do we begin to exercise this kind of generosity in Lent?

Showing Up to Your Neighbor

Woody Allen is quoted as saying, "Eighty percent of success is showing up." The same is true when it comes to showing generosity in Lent. Generosity does not start with a transfer of funds. That is likely only to reinforce feelings of inferiority and shame of the recipient as well as a savior complex of the giver.[2] Generosity in the name of Jesus starts with our personal presence, which allows us to see our neighbors who might otherwise be invisible to us. John Ortberg calls this "the proximity factor." So much comes down to where we spend our time. "Allow yourself to see need," Ortberg writes, "and eventually you'll want to help. Maintain your distance, and you probably won't."[3]

Where do you generally hang out? What roads do you take to work? Which restaurants do you frequent, which parks do you visit, and which neighbors do you notice? With whom do you mingle? Pastor and writer Matt Woodley, in his commentary on Matthew, offers insight on how Jesus hung out with His neighbors:

> Jesus often mingled with *little people*—children,
> women without rights, social misfits such as lepers,

the chronically ill, religious outsiders, tax collectors and prostitutes, and even spiritual wanderers. . . . Our contemporary world is filled with similar groups of people: angry adolescents, unwanted babies, old folks crammed into nursing homes, the mentally ill, moral failures, immigrants. . . . At times in our haste we walk right past them. *They are insubstantial, insignificant and even invisible to us.* Sadly, in the words of an ancient prayer of confession, "We have not heard the cry of the poor and needy"—and sometimes that includes the poor and needy in our own church, neighborhood or home.[4]

For you, Lenten generosity might begin with the weekly discipline of personal presence to the people you are prone to ignore. You might consider walking around your neighborhood, with a friend or two, and ask the Holy Spirit to lead you to take notice and pray for the people on your block. Or you might choose to volunteer at your local library, school, hospital, nursing home, or consignment shop. When someone asks you for money, spend time talking with them. Treat them as an equal. You might even consider taking them to lunch. And if your church has a generosity fund for the needy, contribute as you're able.

Yes, this may be inconvenient. Personal presence is much costlier than simply giving money. My friends Joe and Carrie, who regularly lead mission trips to Southeast Asia, refer to this as having an "interruptible life." Naturally, we Westerners do not appreciate interruptions. But every mundane moment that we love Christ in our neighbor is worthwhile. Before Jesus went to the cross, He charged us to prepare for the judgment day:

When the Son of Man comes in his glory, and all the

angels with him, then he will sit on his glorious throne.
Before him will be gathered all the nations, and he
will separate people one from another as a shepherd
separates the sheep from the goats. And he will place
the sheep on his right, but the goats on the left. Then
the King will say to those on his right, "Come, you who
are blessed by my Father, inherit the kingdom prepared
for you from the foundation of the world. For I was
hungry and you gave me food, I was thirsty and you
gave me drink, I was a stranger and you welcomed me,
I was naked and you clothed me, I was sick and you
visited me, I was in prison and you came to me." Then
the righteous will answer him, saying, "Lord, when did
we see you hungry and feed you, or thirsty and give
you drink? And when did we see you a stranger and
welcome you, or naked and clothe you? And when did
we see you sick or in prison and visit you?" And the
King will answer them, "Truly, I say to you, as you did
it to one of the least of these my brothers, you did it to
me." (Matt. 25:31–40)

Answering Jesus' call to generosity in Lent is simple and
doable. As Woodley explains, "Pay attention, show up, and do
something practical to alleviate the misery of a fellow human
being."[5] Our ordinary, quiet acts of love matter to God and our
neighbor in ways we cannot see in this lifetime.

The Good Friday Gift

In our first year as a church plant, the leaders of Immanuel
Anglican, including AJ and Nancy, gathered to pray during

Holy Week. We asked God to use our church to display Christ's mercy and love to the people of our city. In response to Jesus' generosity toward us, we pooled our resources to give a financial gift to Emmaus Ministries, a Chicago organization that helps men escape survival prostitution and embrace a life of health and wholeness. In the years since, we have repeated this tradition of giving on Good Friday. This helps us exercise generosity in ways that are strategic and corporate. Each year, we identify an agency working on behalf of Christians who minister to those suffering, either locally or around the world. Each year I am amazed at how our congregation gives sacrificially, whether to Nigerians displaced by the violence of Boko Haram or to foster families that adopt children who have been abused.

You too can practice the tradition of a Good Friday gift, whether as an individual, a family, a small group, or a church. Simply budget some money in advance, pray and research agencies that can steward a financial gift responsibly, and give generously—beyond your regular tithe to the local church. This might be a time to highlight and fund your church's current missionary focus. It's also a great time to help the persecuted church. They are our family but often feel forgotten by Christians in the West. A Good Friday gift is a practical, loving way to bridge that gap and express our familial solidarity with them. "As we have opportunity, let us do good to everyone, and *especially to those who are of the household of faith*" (Gal. 6:10, emphasis added).

We might be tempted to pity our brothers and sisters who are jailed or marginalized for their fidelity to Jesus. But they don't ask for our pity. They ask for our prayers. They want to remain faithful to the end and hear Jesus say, "Well done, good and faithful servant" (Matt. 25:21). We have an opportunity to encourage them along the way. With that in mind, I recommend supporting Barnabas Aid (barnabasfund.org), Open Doors USA (opendoorsusa.org), and the Voice of the Martyrs (persecution.com), to name a few. These organizations can help your church learn how to pray for your extended family before you begin giving to them.

Almsgiving is an adventure worth taking and it connects us with others in ways we could never imagine. As we open our hearts, time, and wallets in Lent, Jesus will cause us, well-watered gardens, to overflow for the life of the world.

CHAPTER 11

The Cup of Confession

Several years ago during Lent, Andy was shaking in my office. He couldn't look me in the eye. He wanted to tell me something but was afraid I would judge him for it. After handing him a mug of hot tea, I invited him to sit next to me and I suggested we walk through a short liturgy of confession. Andy hadn't grown up doing anything like this, but he shrugged his shoulders and took my copy of the *Book of Common Prayer*.

Andy read aloud, "I confess to Almighty God . . . that I have sinned by my own fault in thought, word, and deed, in things done and left undone, especially, initiating a long-term sexual relationship with my next door neighbor and hiding it from my church community. For these and all other sins which I cannot now remember, I am truly sorry. I pray to God have mercy on me . . . and ask you for counsel, direction and absolution."

As soon as Andy named his sin with specificity, I could see him breathe a sigh of relief. The shaking stopped, his countenance brightened a touch, and he shared the longer version of his story. We made a plan for repentance, which involved him telling his small group and moving out of his apartment. I then declared the gospel to him from Psalm 103: "The Lord is merciful and gracious, slow to anger and abounding in steadfast love . . . as far as the east is from the west, so far does he remove our transgressions from us."

I then asked the Father to help Andy accept the forgiveness offered to him through Jesus Christ and to give him the strength of the Holy Spirit to walk in obedience. As Andy poured his heart out to his heavenly Father, he cried tears of remorse and joy. Several minutes later, Andy skipped out of my office.

How did Andy go from shaking in fear to skipping in joyful relief? And why does the simple practice of verbal confession to another Christian have such a powerful impact on the soul? I have experienced this process many times, both as one making a confession and as one hearing a confession. I believe the power of restoration comes from the living God who wants us to be free from guilt and shame. And since Lent can be a season of heightened awareness of repentance, it is also a time to learn how to make a personal confession of sin.

But why would we confess our sins to a pastor or Christian friend when we can confess our sins directly to God? Let's look briefly at Scripture as well as a process of confession you can use in your life and ministry.

The Biblical Basis for Confession

The Scriptures teach that confession of sin is like surgery on the soul. God uses it to heal and restore what sin has broken. King David's acknowledgment of his sin turned his torture into joy:

> For when I kept silent, my bones wasted away through my groaning all day long. . . . I acknowledged my sin to you, and I did not cover my iniquity . . . you forgave the

iniquity of my sin. . . . Be glad in the Lord, and rejoice,
O righteous, and shout for joy, all you upright in heart!"
(Ps. 32:3, 5, 11)

The apostle James makes clear that confession should be made not only to God, but also to a fellow Christian: "confess your sins to one another and pray for one another, that you may be healed" (James 5:16). Noticed that James is concerned that we are *healed*, not that we are *punished* or *judged*, which we usually imagine will happen if someone learns of our sin.

In our shame and pride, we are prone to hide our faults from God, our community, and even ourselves. That's why we need to experience the gospel. Lying to ourselves cannot bring peace, but only dangerous isolation. Jesus has already made peace by the blood of His cross (Col. 1:20) and can reconcile us to God and others.

A personal confession of sin is grounded in the truth—telling it, hearing it, and walking joyfully in it. But it also is grounded in God's unconditional love—receiving it, being healed by it, and overflowing with it. Tim Keller articulates how love and truth prepare us to repent of our sins:

> Love without truth is sentimentality; it supports and
> affirms us but keep us in denial about our flaws. Truth
> without love is harshness; it gives us information but
> in such a way that we cannot really hear it. God's
> saving love in Christ, however, is marked by both
> radical truthfulness about who we are and yet also
> radical, unconditional commitment to us. The merciful
> commitment strengthens us to see the truth about
> ourselves and repent. The conviction and repentance
> moves us to cling to rest in God's mercy and grace.[1]

Whether I am confessing sins or hearing a confession, I find it helpful to have a cross in my hand or in my line of sight. This helps me remember the truth and love brought together perfectly for me in Jesus' cross.

The power of forgiveness does not originate with us. However, it does flow through our ministry to each other, since we are Christ's body and empowered by the Holy Spirit (Matt. 18:15–18; Eph. 4:1–32). As we make and hear a verbal confession and receive and pronounce God's forgiveness, the power of the cross is released, applied, and made present.

A Process for Making Confession

First, prepare yourself by confessing to the Lord in private. Give yourself space to interact with Jesus in silence and solitude. Even fifteen minutes goes a long way, although I would recommend more time. Open your soul to the loving, restoring gaze of God. What does He reveal? You might already know what you need to confess, but do not hesitate to let Scripture clarify God's moral call on your life, such as the Ten Commandments (Ex. 20:1–17), Jesus' Sermon on the Mount (Matt. 5–7), Paul's lists of virtues and sins in Ephesians 4:24–5:20, or Jesus' letters to the seven churches in Revelation 2–3.

In his book *Speaking the Truth in Love*, counselor David Powlison provides "X-ray questions" that can prompt honest self-reflection:

- What do you want, desire, crave, lust, and wish for?
- Where do you find refuge, comfort, escape, security?
- How do you implicitly say, "if only . . ." (to get what you want)?

• Whom must you please? Whose opinion of you counts?[2]

I sometimes use a journal so I can capture the reflections and insights from this process. The point is that the Holy Spirit will use this time of silent, Scripture-soaked meditation to prepare you for the next step.

Second, confess to a mature Christian of the same gender whom you respect. This might be a mentor, pastor, or counselor. I confess to my bishop and my spiritual director, both of whom are spiritual fathers to me. In any case, you are looking for someone who can be Christ's ambassador of reconciliation (2 Cor. 5). As such, their personal presence should approximate Christ's truth and love to you. Richard Foster recommends confessing to someone with "spiritual maturity, wisdom, compassion, good common sense, an ability to keep confidence, and a wholesome sense of humor."[3]

If you are confessing to a peer, choose someone who is strong yet safe. They need to be strong in that they can remain separate from you and your confession. They also need to be safe in that they can show empathy rather than steamroll you with advice. And they need to keep everything confidential. I have a few trusted friends in my life whom I call or seek out for confession.

Third, be thorough in your confession. This can surely be embarrassing. You might find yourself wanting to manage the other person's opinion of you by holding back the full truth. Be aware that indirect and vague language is not confession: "I have been struggling lately," "I messed up again," "I got triggered." Or you might be inclined to hide behind spiritual or psychological jargon. Resist these temptations by naming your sin against God with specificity. This is your chance to be known, loved, and forgiven in the "secret heart" (Ps. 51:6).

Fourth, receive God's forgiveness. When your pastor or friend declares the gospel to you, respond in agreement, either silently or aloud. Praise God for His love for you in Christ and walk in freedom. You may not feel free. In fact, you may not feel anything but shame for a while. But know that in Christ your sin has been forgiven, though it may take time to sink in for you.

A Process for Hearing Confession

First, live a confessional life. There is no substitute for preparing you to minister the gospel than experiencing it yourself. Confessing your own sins will give you the humility necessary to hear others confess theirs. "If anyone is caught in any transgression, you who are spiritual should restore him in a spirit of gentleness. *Keep watch on yourself*, lest you too be tempted" (Gal. 6:1, emphasis added). You who are spiritual need to keep watch on yourself, even as you lead others through restoration. Using the confessional as a way to feel superior is toxic. We must remember our own depravity and complete dependence on Christ's atoning work for us. For this reason, the Anglican confessional liturgy ends with the pastor saying, "Pray for me, a sinner."[4]

Offer a general invitation to hear a confession. Let the people in your church or community know that you are willing to hear confessions, and then let them take the initiative. No one should be tricked, forced or guilt-tripped into making a confession. My church employs this motto when it comes to making a confession: "None must, some should, all can."

Begin the meeting by inviting them to confess their sins. You might begin with a prayer like I used with Andy: "The Lord be in your heart and upon your lips that you may truly and humbly confess your sins: In the Name of the Father, and of the Son, and of the Holy Spirit, *Amen*."[5] Or you might begin with a Scripture like 1 Timothy 1:15: "The saying is trustworthy and deserving of full acceptance, that Christ Jesus came into the world to save sinners, of whom I am the foremost."

Listen to their confession with patience, compassion, and wisdom. Whether they are using a liturgy, pouring out their heart extemporaneously, or some combination of the two, let them name their sin. Do not confess for them. You may need to draw out the full confession, especially if they are having difficulty: "Is there anything else you would like to confess to God?" You might become aware of their patterns of thinking or behaving that need to be addressed with practical actions. For now, pray about that silently as you continue to listen.

Intercede for them on the spot. I usually ask the individual to stand up for this. With their permission, I will pray for them with my hand on their back or shoulder. After praying for the Holy Spirit to strengthen and comfort them, I prompt the individual to confess to the Father what they just confessed to me.

Finally, proclaim the gospel. Be prepared for this. The confessing individual will be hungry for a gospel meal, with full servings of hope, grace, and peace! When the law of God reveals our sin, we are most ready to hear the precious truth that the Son of God has removed our sin. Remind the individual that they are God's child: adopted, forgiven, filled with the Holy Spirit, called to serve King Jesus, possessing an inheritance that will never fade. Remind them that when we confess our sins, God is faithful and just to forgive us and cleanse us from all unrighteousness (1 John 1:9). And that if anyone sins, we have an advocate with the Father, Jesus Christ (1 John 2:1–2)

Everything shared in this conversation is to remain confidential. Their confession must not be a topic of conversation offline between you and another person. However, there are several exceptions to be made for their sake and yours:

- If they give you permission to share their confession with another pastor or caregiver, you may do so to help others understand how to best care for them.
- If they are planning to hurt themselves or someone else, you need to notify the proper authorities.
- If they have abused another person in any way, you need to prompt them to turn themselves into the police, and you need to fill out a police report.[6]

Like the Lenten fast, the process of confession is not designed to cure addictions, medical conditions, or mental illness of any kind. You may need to refer them to a recovery program or a medical professional. Neither does this process exist in isolation from the journey of discipleship. It may also be appropriate to draft a plan for active repentance that involves the larger community. When you and I find ourselves like Andy, isolated in our sin and shaking in fear, we need to hear the liberating, loving truth from John in the context of Christian community:

> This is the message we have heard from him and proclaim to you, that God is light, and in him is no darkness at all. If we say we have fellowship with him while we walk in darkness, we lie and do not practice the truth. But if we walk in the light, as he is in the light, we have fellowship with one another, and the blood of Jesus his Son cleanses us from all sin. (1 John 1:5–7)

Jesus' love and truth has power to heal us, cleanse us, and restore us to joyful fellowship with God and neighbor. And confession is a powerful way to encounter that.

CHAPTER 12

Tying It All Together

Hopefully you started to capture a vision for walking with Christ in Lent. But you might feel overwhelmed by all that God could do in your life during this season. Take a deep breath and consider the larger picture. Remember that the Lord is shaping you for His purposes over a lifetime (Phil. 1:6). We cannot rush the process, but only take it one day and one season at a time.

Let's look at how to tie together everything we've discussed so you can make a simple, workable plan for the upcoming season of Lent.[1]

Ask God for Vision

As you consider the forty-day journey ahead, what is the Lord's invitation to you? Spend a few moments in prayer and ask the Holy Spirit to give you a simple yet compelling picture of the change He wants for you. Think about what we have covered in the book so far to reflect on what God may be calling you to. Perhaps He's calling you to cultivate a greater hunger for God. Or maybe He's asking you to take on the yoke of Jesus' humility. Perhaps He wants to fill you with joy on Easter Sunday and recapture your imagination with His love. Maybe you need to learn how to submit your sexual appetite to Jesus Christ. Or maybe He wants you to grow in compassion and generosity, to fight for the needs of the poor and oppressed.

Just spend some time with an open Bible and an open heart, asking God to point out one specific way that He wants to train you to become like Christ during Lent. You could start with Jesus' Sermon on the Mount in Matthew 5–7, or the list of the fruit of the Spirit in Galatians 5:22–23. Write down the ideas that come to your mind, and then share them with your pastor, small group leader, spouse, or a Christian friend you trust. You can ask them to pray with you to narrow it down to one specific area.

Be Honest about Your Inner Rebel

What part of you does not like Lent and resists this vision for Christlikeness? For instance, if your sexual appetite is never denied, part of you will hate submitting it to a lord of any kind. Or if you are afraid of situations you cannot control, surrendering them to a Father will spark an internal battle. What part of you resents the wilderness ahead? Once you've pinpointed your inner rebel, admit it to yourself and verbalize it.

Alice is one of the leaders who helped me start Immanuel Anglican. She finds that she is better prepared for Lent when she recognizes her "inner saboteur" in advance. "I don't like Lent," she admits. "My heart thrills with the thought of Easter, but I groan when I think about Lent, because I hate failure." Alice finds that even small-level fasts, such as forgoing cream in her coffee, exposes her personal weakness. Despite her best efforts and planning, she can't keep a perfect fast. And that drives the self-sufficient part of her crazy.

Even as Alice is transparent about her perfectionist side that hates Lent, she also affirms the childlike, trusting side of her that welcomes Lent as a means to draw nearer to her Savior: "The Lord uses my failure to shatter my pride, which brings me back to the reality that I am dust and need the Lord's mercy every moment of my life."

I can relate to Alice's internal struggle. I love feeling the energy and comfort of being well-fed, and I like myself better when I am happy. That's why my inner rebel hates the fasting and bodily weakness associated with Lent. I don't like the grouchy, low-energy version of myself. The more honest I am about that, the fewer excuses I find to avoid fasting when Lent approaches. And the more I submit my body to Jesus, the more transforming work He can do in me.

We need to ask ourselves, "What part of me is ready for this? And what part of me is not ready for this?" Identify your inner objections, doubts, and secret plans to reject God's invitation to you. The more self-reflective and honest you can be about your inner rebel that resists His work, the less powerful will that inner rebel be. And this sort of honesty will free you to say, "Yes, Jesus, I want this. I need this. I choose this."

Choose Your Disciplines

Finally, choose the means that the Lord will use to best help you realize His vision for you. Thankfully, as we have discussed, we have some historic, time-tested means, so you don't have to start from scratch. We all can practice fasting, prayer, and generosity in some form or another.[2] Make sure that your Lenten disciplines help you walk toward God's plan for you, and be sure to stay connected to your Christian community. You need support not just in choosing your Lenten practices, but also in maintaining them and getting back on track when you fail.

All the historic disciplines of Lent are fruitful. The Lord will use them to change your character and make you holy. This is a slow affair, to be sure. Biblical scholar N. T. Wright finds the process to be downright agricultural:

> Character is a slowly forming thing. You can no more force character on someone than you can force a tree to produce fruit when it isn't ready to do so. The person has to choose, again and again, to develop the moral muscle and skills which will shape and form the fully flourishing character.[3]

As I write this book, my current vision, apart from Lent, for growth in Christlikeness is to become so filled with Jesus' patience that it overflows to my children when they most need it from me. Instead of fulminating with irritation, I want to overflow with patient love for them when circumstances at home become stressful. My intention is strengthened when I affirm that this is a better way to live, and when I admit that I am tempted to spend most of my energy at work and give my kids the leftovers. The means I have chosen include memorizing and meditating on Ephesians 3:14–21, setting boundaries with my work to preserve energy for home, and confessing my sins to a close friend and to my spiritual director.

The paradox is that this plan leaves fewer things in my control. This is to be expected, and this is why Lent can be intimidating. Growing in Christlikeness, especially during Lent, is a process of surrender to Jesus' grand undertaking of renewing all things by the Word of His power, including our rebellious selves. Without God's grace for our failure and weakness, we would be toast by lunchtime on Ash Wednesday. But "he who did not spare his own Son . . . will he not also with him graciously give us all things?" (Rom. 8:32).

Expect to live fully and deeply in God's grace during Lent.

PART 3

LEADING

OTHERS

THROUGH

LENT

CHAPTER 13

Leading Children through Lent

This chapter is written for parents who are seeking to lead their kids through Lent. Yet it's also meant to encourage and equip grandparents, Sunday school teachers, children's ministry directors, and anyone else who has spiritual influence in the lives of children. In it I hope you find creative ideas and encouragement for leading children through the glorious season of Lent.

You Are Not a Failure

Most parents I know feel guilty about what they are not providing for their kids. Some are concerned they aren't giving their children enough time and personal attention. Others conclude they aren't providing enough educational and enrichment opportunities. What are you not providing enough for your kids? Organic nutrition, protection from a bully, family vacations, college tuition? As a city parent, I feel guilty for not getting my kids outside to play and exercise more often.

For some parents, guilt and anxiety push them to push their kids harder to win at life—in school, sports, extracurricular activities, even church activities. On the outside, that seems to work for a while, but resentment and fear inevitably grow on the inside of the child. The process then either backfires or repeats itself in the next generation.

For others, parental guilt triggers discouragement: "I've tried and failed so many times that it's not worth it." I believe this is why many Christian families have quit family devotions. They tried to start several times, but it did not seem to take. Life got chaotic, or the siblings started fighting during prayer time, or the parents just forgot to keep at it. Many who began with high aspirations for consistent family devotions feel like failures.

Be assured: *You are not a failure!* If you still have children under your roof, keep sowing seeds of the gospel. The harvest comes a long time from now. Trial and error are to be expected. Starting, stopping, and restarting dozens or hundreds of times are part of the package. The next season of Lent can be an opportunity for you to restart your family devotional life. One of my friends with several teenagers recently said to me, "Kids are forgiving and forgetful. If you begin an annual tradition with your elementary age child now, they will assume they have 'always done it' by the time they are grown."

Here are four ways to gain traction in leading your family through the season of Lent. (If your kids are old enough, you might consider letting them read this chapter and then suggest their own ideas for practicing Lent.)

Make It Sustainable

Lent is forty days. That's a long time for families. So instead of attempting forty devotional times with your family, aim for a fifteen- or twenty-minute devotional time once a week after a family meal. That adds up to six family devotional times in six weeks, with a rough total of ninety minutes of spiritual conversation. Can you manage that? If so, make room for screaming, eye-rolling, and random comments about poop.

Here are some ways you can use that time:

Read the Bible and pray.[1] You can start by reading from the Gospels, focusing on Jesus' teaching and passion. Discuss what the passage means for our life and then spend a few minutes praying together as a family. For younger kids, you might consider reading stories from *The Big Picture Bible* (for ages two to six), *The Jesus Storybook Bible* (ages six to ten), or *The Action Bible*, a Bible formatted like a graphic novel (for ages eight to thirteen).

Use *The Book of Common Prayer for Kids* (available for free at aarondamiani.com/resources). This resource—from Resurrection Church South Austin in Texas—is built upon prayers from *The Book of Common Prayer* and contains helpful tips and pictures. The format is also more accessible for children.

Work through a catechism. Spend a few minutes exploring one to two catechism questions with your children in order to help them better understand the fundamental teachings of the faith, especially those that relate to themes emphasized in Lent—such as sin, repentance, forgiveness, God's law, and the good news. Help them memorize the answers to the questions and be able to explain them in their own words. (I've included a list of helpful catechisms on pages 153–54.)

Read a Lent devotional and pray. Reading through a devotional is a simple way to teach your children biblical truths in an accessible manner. I recommend you select one with shorter daily readings so you don't overwhelm your kids. After the reading, discuss how the content connects to our life and then pray together.

I am so grateful that my grandmother read Scripture at the breakfast table to my father and his brother. Neither of them could have cared less at the time, and they even tried to ignore her. And my grandfather was opposed to her doing this. Years later, those awkwardly planted seeds gave way to a great gospel growth in both of her son's lives. My grandmother never saw that harvest in her lifetime but had faith to keep sowing seeds. "Let us not grow weary of doing good, for in due season we will reap, if we do not give up" (Gal. 6:9).

Make It Instructional

Lent is a learning opportunity for kids, adults, Sunday school teachers, and youth workers alike. I encourage you to devote a portion of your time during family devotions or children's church to teach everyone about Lent.

Teach them the purpose of Lent. As soon as you decide to practice Lent in your family or children's ministry, teach everyone involved about the compelling purpose for the season: to become like Jesus and to walk closely with Him. If you have a personalized vision for Lent (see chapter 12), share that with them. You can help them "own" the season of Lent for themselves by asking them why and how they practice it.

Teach them the history of Lent. As I mentioned in chapters 1–3, the history of Lent is wrapped up in the story of Jesus, which begins in the Old Testament. Here are a few ideas for teaching salvation history:

- Reading aloud the accounts of the forty-day fasts (Moses in Exodus 34, Elijah in 1 Kings 19, and Jesus in Matthew 4) and the passion narratives.
- Read the accounts of the forty years in the wilderness from the Pentateuch. For older children, you can compare and contrast the wilderness wanderings with Jesus' forty days in the wilderness to teach them how Jesus is true and faithful Israel, how he succeeded where Israel failed.
- Ask them to imagine what it was like to fast in secret on Good Friday while under persecution (see chapter 2), and then teach them how God gives us strength to endure trials and temptations of all kinds.

Teach them the theology of Lent. Catechism questions are a great way to impart to children the theological foundations of the Christian faith. They can be recited and discussed at the dinner table, at children's church, or in a classroom setting. I recommend the Anglican catechism *To Be a Christian* (available for free download at aarondamiani.com/resources) or the *New City Catechism* (available for free at newcitycatechism.com). Here's a sample from *To Be a Christian*:

> *What is the Gospel?* The Gospel is the good news of God loving and saving lost mankind through the ministry in word and deed of his Son, Jesus Christ. (1 Cor. 15:1–4; Rom. 5:15; John 1:12; 1 John 5:11–12)

> *Why did Jesus suffer?* Jesus suffered for our sins so we could have peace with God, as prophesied in the Old Testament: "But he was pierced for our transgressions;

he was crushed for our iniquities; upon him was the chastisement that brought us peace, and with his wounds we are healed." (Isa. 53:5)

What does it mean for you to repent? To repent means that I have a change of heart, turning from sinfully serving myself to serving God as I follow Jesus Christ. I need God's help to make this change. (Acts 2:38; 3:19)[2]

Make It Tangible

A child's attention span and memory skyrocket when you make a lesson tangible. Here are a few ways to make Lent a tactile and multisensory experience:

Lent Devotional Candles. Let's be honest: kids like fire. And candles can symbolize the light of Christ to family members of every age. You can use this to help your family mark the weeks and create a sense of progression toward Easter.

Place six purple candles on your family dinner table. On the first week of your family devotions, light one of the candles. On the second week, light an additional candle so that two candles are lit during devotions. On the third week, three candles, and so on (similar to an Advent wreath). You can even add a seventh candle (white or rose colored) to symbolize Easter. On Easter morning, light all the candles to celebrate Jesus' victory over death. You can even let your kids decorate or create one or more of the candles before Lent.

A Lenten Seed. At the beginning of Lent, plant a seed inside a clear cup. Let a different member of your family water it every day at the dinner table. As you watch it grow, reflect with your children on how Lent is a season of dying to self and awakening to new life in the Spirit.[3] Use this time to discuss Jesus' invitation to death and resurrection in John 12:24: "Truly, truly, I say to you, unless a grain of wheat falls into the earth and dies, it remains alone; but if it dies, it bears much fruit."

The Bitter Cup.[4] On Maundy Thursday or Good Friday, read the passion narrative together as a family. Mix vinegar and grape juice together in a cup and let every family member take a sip, to symbolize how Jesus drank the cup of wrath.

Good Friday Shroud. Put up a wooden cross at home. During Holy Week, drape the cross with black cloth. Invite your kids to write down their sins on pieces of paper and pin them on the black cloth to symbolize how Jesus takes and forgives our sins. Before the kids wake up on Easter Sunday, remove the black cloth and all the "sins" and replace it with a white cloth to symbolize that Christ is risen and that our sins are taken away—forever.

The Easter Mountain.[5] Noel and John Piper made an "Easter Mountain" with their young children to depict the events of Holy Week. In their book *Treasuring God in Our Traditions*, Noel recommends using play dough for the mountain—including a "cave" for the burial, a rock to cover the cave, and a cross on top of the mountain—and chenille sticks for stick figures. You can allow each child to have a stick figure to roleplay the passion narrative during Holy Week.

Make It Sacrificial

One of the most meaningful things you could do as a family during Lent is make a common sacrifice. The trick is to *invite* rather than *force* your kids to join you in this. Prayer, fasting, and almsgiving can all be scaled to your child's capacity and shared as a family.

Here are a few ideas:

Host a Soup Night once a week. Instead of eating a full-course meal, make soup using the leftovers in your pantry and fridge. You could turn this into a family activity by inviting your kids to help you make the soup and some homemade bread. You can then use the money you saved to help a needy family. As you eat, teach your kids about the "true fast" that God requires in Isaiah 58:6–7: "Is not this the fast that I choose . . . to share your bread with the hungry?"

Invite your kids to join you in abstaining from a luxury. This will be tough for your little ones, but invite them to abstain from a treat such as dessert or screen-based entertainment. Use the money you saved to sponsor a child with an organization like Kids Alive International or Compassion International. You can make this even more tangible by giving each child the cash value of their sacrifice in coins, which they can place into a common pouch or basket to collect for the donation. Pray together each week for the child your family sponsors.

Teach younger kids (seven and up) how to "make a chocolate banana smoothie" of prayer. This is a fun, metaphorical way to teach them how to study the Bible on their own for spiritual growth. What I am describing below is a spiritual activity, which teaches them the joyful discipline of personal prayer and Bible study during Lent, although you could make a literal smoothie to enjoy together. Here is the recipe:

One "frozen banana" of my life right now. This

"ingredient" is where the child journals or draws their current life experience: what's bothering them, their fears, hurts, hopes, and frustrations.

One "half-cup of Nutella" of God's loving truth. Help your child find a verse or passage of Scripture that speaks to their current life situation. Some good starting points are: Proverbs, Psalms, Philippians, 1 Peter, and 1 John. Teach them to ask God to use this passage to instruct, comfort, or warn them. They can journal or draw their reflections.

Blend and share the "smoothie." Give them a few minutes to ask the Holy Spirit to help them digest this loving truth. And then share your "smoothies" with each other by describing how God spoke to you through His Word. Yes, this works for adults also! And your kids will be more enthusiastic in doing this if you are leading by example—and probably if literal smoothies are involved.

If the Lord has seen fit to give you responsibility over children, take the opportunity to lead them through Lent. No one does this perfectly. None of us even comes close. Sow seeds of the gospel in these forty days, and in time the Lord will reap a harvest in generations to come.

CHAPTER 14

Leading Churches through Lent

If you are a church leader—a pastor, elder, worship leader, staff member, small group leader, or anyone else with influence in the life of your church—and are wondering how to lead others through Lent, this chapter outlines specific practices that you can use or improvise on. No matter what kind of congregation you lead, and whatever your role in shaping it, I hope to resource you with historic yet fresh ideas for leading your church through the season of Lent.

The Importance of Going First

I will never forget saying goodbye to the church in which I served as an assistant pastor. As a full-time church planting resident, I had an opportunity to preach once a month for three years. I took this responsibility seriously and worked diligently to prepare and craft each sermon for maximum spiritual impact. Each time, I prayed for spiritual fruit to be produced. As my time drew to an end and the congregation said their goodbyes, a few people mentioned my preaching in passing. But, to my surprise, the most common refrain was about my parenting. I heard things like: "I was blessed to watch you be a father to your kids in church," and "I appreciate the way you and Laura work together to raise your family."

What? Honestly, fathering my kids during and after church had been a far-from-perfect afterthought. Handing out fruit snacks, shushing a fussy toddler, smiling and nodding at their Sunday school coloring page—why did people appreciate simple gestures like those? What about what I thought were mind-blowing word studies, poignant introductions, and life-changing applications?

All that mattered less than I assumed for one simple reason: the people of God are looking for examples. They want their leaders to show them how to follow Jesus, even as we teach them. Challenging sermons and correct doctrine matter a great deal, but are inseparable from a godly life. The people we teach and exhort need to see us fail, repent, obey, and live by the power of the Spirit to love God and others. Another way of saying it is that our three-dimensional lives are usually more interesting than our two-dimensional sermons.

Peter exhorts us to shepherd our churches by "being examples to the flock" (1 Peter 5:3). Paul was an example to the young Corinthian believers who needed a spiritual father: "Be imitators of me, as I am of Christ" (1 Cor. 11:1). When so many false apostles relied on their rhetoric to lead the Corinthians, Paul ministered Jesus through his sincere, openhanded presence in their community (2 Cor. 2:14–3:3).

The most important way for you to lead your church through the season of Lent is to show them with your life. You need to go first. Church leaders are far from perfect, to be sure. But we are called to lead with our lives. We cannot expect our people to devote themselves to Jesus in Lent at a level that we are not.

With that in mind, consider how you might lead your church by example.

If your church does not currently practice Lent, consider observing it yourself this year. Hold off on leading the whole church, or group, for now. Practice fasting, prayer, and generosity at a level that challenges you. You can ask your most trusted leaders to join you and to support each other through the season. Write down the lessons you learn so that you can share them with others you pastor or lead.

Intercede for your church. Ask the Father to prepare the way for them to draw near to Jesus in Lent and Easter. Pray for your leaders, staff, or small group members by name.

Ensure you are being pastored and led. In the words credited to Saint Teresa of Avila, "The person who has himself as a spiritual director has a fool for director." With that in mind, seek out a spiritual mentor who can encourage and challenge you during Lent. Ideally, this person will be able to handle hearing a confession of sins from you (see chapter 11). That might be someone you already know and trust, like your local church pastor, district superintendent, bishop, local spiritual director, or another leader you know. Do not hesitate to reach out to a group that offers quality pastoral care to pastors, like Pastor Serve (www.pastorserve.net) or Soul Shepherding (soulshepherding.org).

Increase your personal giving during Lent. Be truly sacrificial to express your love for Jesus and your commitment to His bride and mission.

Give extended time to prayer and preparation during Holy Week. As Holy Week approaches, you can prepare for the week by prayerfully meditating on passages that depict Jesus' passion. This is especially helpful for those who will preside over or preach during Holy Week services. (See the appendix for specific suggestions.)

Once you have followed Jesus on the forty-day journey of Lent, He may ask you to take others along with you next time. Here are a few ideas to consider as you shape your church's outreach, discipleship, preaching, and worship in Lent. And please consider asking your staff or leaders to read this chapter—or the entire book—before making final decisions.

Lenten Outreach Ideas

I have included this first because outreach is sometimes ignored during Lent. It need not be an afterthought, though, since Lent trains us to reach out to and love our neighbors in Jesus' name. Here are ways to face outward as a church during Lent:

Shrove Tuesday pancake night. Shrove Tuesday is the final day before Lent. For many Christians around the world, it is a time to clean rich foods out of the house by serving delicious pancakes to their neighbors. That's why some call this day "Pancake Tuesday." You can organize a Shrove Tuesday pancake night by asking your leaders and small groups to host a neighborhood pancake night in their homes.

Stations of the Cross. During Holy Week, you can host a biblically based Stations of the Cross art exhibit for the community. Last year, our church commissioned artists within and outside our church to create fourteen pieces depicting Jesus' passion, from His prayer in Gethsemane to His body being placed in the tomb. We distributed invitations all over the city for people to join us for refreshments and reflection. (See the appendix for more information about the Stations of the Cross.)

Good Friday gift. Consider using Lent as a time to highlight and fund the missionary focus of your church, whether it is foster care, an unreached people group, or human trafficking. Call people to fast and pray for this ministry during Lent, and collect a special offering on Good Friday. This is an excellent way for the classic disciplines of Lent—fasting, prayer, and generosity—to point your church outward.

Easter festival. From the perspective of the church calendar, this is not technically a Lenten outreach event. From the perspective of your planning and the church's momentum, it might as well be. Use Easter Sunday to reach out to your community. This starts with an inviting and well-planned worship service. If you have that covered, consider throwing a festival for the surrounding community with fun activities that kids will enjoy, such as a bounce castle, an Easter egg hunt, and face painting.

Lenten Worship Ideas

The appendix provides specifics on the liturgy and logistics for special services in Lent, but here are several ways in which you might want to lead your church through Lent in worship:

Ash Wednesday service. This is a low-overhead, high-yield service that any church can pull off. Ash Wednesday gives your church a chance to begin Lent in a spirit of prayerful repentance.

Holy Week services. Most churches observe at least one of the Holy Week services: Good Friday. If you have the bandwidth, I would encourage you to add at least one more, such as Maundy Thursday, or changing up a service you already celebrate, like Palm Sunday.

Tastefully use darker colors in your worship space. Colors like purple and black are visual reminders of Jesus' suffering and our repentance. Typically, Lenten fabrics are matte finish and coarse, such as burlap or linen. You can drape fabric across the front of your worship space, communion table, and cross. You might tear fabric instead of cutting it in order to visualize the torn garments of repentance. On Good Friday, you can use a large fabric panel that is black, overlaid with torn strips of gray fabric with black abstract shapes printed on it.

Simplify your worship space. Consider removing other art elements, be it liturgical or otherwise. Less is more during Lent, so strip out whatever you can. What stands out is the lack of liturgical art elements where you normally have them the rest of the year. For evening services—Ash Wednesday, Maundy Thursday, and Good Friday—you can use low lighting to create a somber mood.

Art cards. At Immanuel, we ask artists in the congregation to create art, or find a piece of art they have already created, to accompany a Scripture text for a certain Sunday in Lent. These are printed on quality, thick paper or cardstock with the Scripture reference and artist's name on the reverse. The small cards are included in the Sunday bulletin. Sometimes they serve as a reflection of sorts, with space for notes and prayers on the reverse side.

Choose songs that fit the Lenten season. Select the songs that are mournful, repentant, and prompt reflection on Jesus' suffering, such as "*Kyrie Eleison*/Lord Have Mercy" (traditional), Psalm 126, "When I Survey the Wondrous Cross" (Watts), "Jesus, Remember Me" (Taize Community), "Take, O Take Me As I Am" (Bell), "The Power of the Cross" (Getty & Townsend),

"Lord, Who Throughout These Forty Days" (Hernaman), "In Christ Alone" (Getty), and "Draw Me Nearer" (Crosby).

Lead people in corporate confession. Toward the beginning of your worship services, lead your people in a time of silent confession, and then invite them to pray a written liturgical confession—either written in your service program or displayed on the screen. You can write your own, but I recommend using an older prayer that has stood the test of time. Do not forget to assure your people of the gospel when the confession is complete!

Lenten Preaching Ideas

Lent is one of my favorite times to preach. The season creates an environment of holy receptivity to the Word of God. Preachers have six Sundays to work with, plus special services like Ash Wednesday, Maundy Thursday, and Good Friday. If you are solely responsible for the preaching at your church—I see you, church planters and small church pastors!—consider raising up a promising lay preacher or bringing in a guest preacher for some of these services. You need to preserve enough stamina to last you through Easter weekend.

Here are some ways to preach during Lent:

Preach from the lectionary. The lectionary is a prescribed set of Scripture readings for each Sunday according to the church calendar. You can see the lectionary readings for the coming weeks and years at http://lectionary.library.vanderbilt.edu.

Preach a series devoted to the themes of Lent. A five-part sermon series will cover all the Sundays in Lent except for Palm Sunday, which you might want to set on its own. A seven-part sermon series could include Ash Wednesday and Palm Sunday. Some sermon series to consider are: the Seven Deadly Sins, Following Jesus into the Wilderness, the Meaning of the Cross, or Jesus' Letters to the Churches in Revelation 2–3. You might also consider a series of expository preaching on Isaiah, Mark, Philippians, the Psalms of Lament, or James.

Lenten Discipleship Ideas

As we discovered in chapter 2, the disciplines of Lent are some of the earliest ways the church made disciples of Jesus. Invite those who are ready and willing to join you in your journey to Easter in these ways:

Teach your people about Lent before the season is upon you. In the six to eight weeks leading up to Lent—usually January and February—invite your small groups or leadership team to prepare for Lent with this book or another. Discipleship happens when people are actually making changes in their lives, which takes instruction and planning.

Recommend a Lent devotional. I recommend you not write one unless you have the bandwidth. Generating it on your own takes a great deal of time and effort. *From the Grave: A 40 Day Lent Devotional* by A. W. Tozer and *Bread and Wine,* a compilation of readings for Lent and Easter from famous writers in history, are great resources, to name only a couple.

Offer spiritual direction and confession. You can make this available on Ash Wednesday, Good Friday, and set hours in your week.

Host a small group. Encourage your people to gather in small groups to fast, pray, and be generous together.

Morning and Evening Prayer. Appoint a leader to lead

Morning or Evening Prayer (as outlined in the *Book of Common Prayer*) in their home, your church, or a local diner.

Lead a baptism class. Hold a class one Sunday or one evening during the week where you teach the portions of a catechism or key doctrines of Christianity.

BONUS TIPS

Start planning early. Plan your Lenten services and ministries at least four to six weeks before Ash Wednesday for maximum impact.

Be patient with yourself. Learning how to lead people through Lent comes from failure, awkward moments, and years of trial and error.

Take the long view with your church. Build your Lent traditions one year at a time. Forming Christians is slow and deep work.

Keep the vision front and center. Why are you practicing Lent as a congregation? What would be lost if you did not observe the season? Use part 1 of this book to help you clarify the spiritual outcomes you are working toward, and then communicate them at every turn.

Align key leaders and staff. All the resources spent developing unity and a sense of shared mission is worthwhile. You will need their spiritual and strategic support during the intensity of Lent and Holy Week.

Spiritual leadership of the local church is a great privilege. The very Lord of the Universe has committed this holy assignment to us and given us His Spirit to see us through. Let us take up our mantle of leading our church through Lent by praying, planning, and inviting our congregation to follow us as we follow Christ.

CHAPTER 15

Conclusion

L ast night, my sister-in-law Mary Margaret (my wife's sister) got engaged to a wonderful man. Her fiancé, Gabe, had planned a secret gathering of her family and friends to toast the occasion, which Laura and I hosted in our Chicago apartment. We happen to live near Wrigley Field, and the Cubs were playing, so traffic was horrible. In order to make it for the dinner, the toasting, and the in-person engagement story, most of the guests had to endure a long, torturous journey during rush hour. Then they had to find parking, locate our building, and walk up the stairs. There was no gilded path to the engagement party.

But they made it.

And let me tell you, we feasted! The brisket and sweet corn—and even the Brussels sprouts—were sumptuous. I ate more than I should have. The engagement story was riveting, and the ring sparkled. Guests took turns toasting—and roasting—the future bride and groom, with our anticipation growing for the wedding feast to come. By the time dessert and coffee were served, everyone seemed to have forgotten their stressful journey. Mary Margaret and Gabe were just engaged, making the trip totally worthwhile.

After reading this book, the forty days of Lent might seem

intimidating to you. Now that you know that there is no gilded path to Easter Sunday, you might be weighing your options. Or maybe you are in the middle of Lent right now and want out.

Friend, let me encourage you: there is a feast awaiting you at Easter and in heaven. It's worth the discomfort, the uncertainty, and the personal exposure that comes with observing Lent. You're an expected guest around the table, and the celebration will make the suffering seem inconsequential.

Don't forget the vision! Our Lord Jesus is using the season of Lent to form us into His image, corporately and individually. For some readers, He's reshaping your imagination to reflect His holiness. For others, He's working a beautiful humility into your character. Some of us need to learn how to repent of sins during Lent and experience the freedom it brings. Others need to cultivate a different, healthier relationship to food, drink, and entertainment. Rejoice! Our desires, habits, and pocketbooks are being aligned with the kingdom of God. We are being set free. The Lord of the church is washing us with His Word, preparing us for glory, one day and one Lent at a time. And that's why it's good to give up.

Appendix
Special Services in Lent

In this overview of the special services in Lent, I have sought to make "mere Christian" resources available to anyone who wishes to receive them. No matter what denomination you belong to, you can use whatever you find here that best serves the mission of your church. If I share aspects of the Anglican way for how to celebrate these services, it is only to be transparent, not to push my tradition onto you. If you're in a high-church context, you will need more instruction than I have provided here. I have included the liturgies we use at Immanuel at aarondamiani.com/resources.

Ash Wednesday

Why do we celebrate it? Ash Wednesday helps us begin the season of Lent with repentant, humble hearts and to place our hope in Jesus' death and resurrection for salvation. We celebrate Ash Wednesday to be reminded of our mortality and need for God's mercy in an ancient and biblical way.

How do we celebrate it? Ash Wednesday is a simple prayer service which can include the imposition of ashes onto the foreheads of the people who come forward. You can hold this service any time of the day. Some churches choose to expand this service to include communion, though that is unnecessary.

What is the order of service? The basic liturgy for Ash Wednesday is as follows:

- Opening Prayer
- Scripture readings[1] and sermon
- An invitation to the season of Lent and to receive the imposition of ashes
- Distribution of the ashes
- A song of repentance (traditionally the *Kyrie*)
- Reading of Psalm 51
- Repeat the song of repentance (again, the *Kyrie* works best)
- Public prayers of confession (sometimes referred to as a "litany")
- A closing song
- Benediction
- An exchange of peace

For more details on the Anglican liturgy for Ash Wednesday, pick up a copy of the *Book of Common Prayer* (1979).

Where do I get the ashes? You can buy them from church supply stores or make them yourself on the days leading up to Ash Wednesday. Traditionally, the ashes are made by burning the palm branches from last year's Palm Sunday service. If you do not have or cannot obtain palm branches, simply use brown paper bags or white paper without coatings or dyes. Burn the palm branches or paper outside using a metal garbage can or receptacle. Scoop the ashes into a strainer, with a bowl underneath. Smash the ashes gently against the strainer with a brush or pestle. This will separate the finer ash from the coarser pieces. Distribute the finer ash, which you will use in the service, into small bowls for use in the service. Ceramic or glass bowls work great; they just need to be small enough to be held in one hand. Keep these bowls on a small table that you can access easily during the service. Also, include a few lemon wedges, a pitcher of water, a towel, and an empty bowl—all of which you will need for clean-up. Right before the service begins, drizzle a small amount of olive oil, which works much better than water, around the inner rim of the bowl. This will come in handy when it comes time to administer the ashes (see below).

How do I administer the ashes? First, have another pastor or a deacon administer ashes onto your forehead. If you have a large congregation, you may need to form two or more stations. Ushers can invite people to come forward, either row by row or as they are ready. They can either kneel or stand to receive the ashes.

When it comes time to administer the ashes, wet your thumb with a bit of oil, and then coat your thumb with ashes. (You can repeat this as often as needed.) Make a cross on their forehead, first with a vertical line and then with a horizontal line. As you do that, say to them, "Remember, oh man, that you are dust, and to dust you shall return." You can then add, "Repent and believe the gospel," or "But for the grace of Christ." (To clean the ashes off your hands, squeeze the lemon juice on your fingers, and then rinse with water.)

Palm Sunday

Why do we celebrate it? Palm Sunday is the day we live the memory of Jesus' triumphal entry into Jerusalem as the conquering and humble King (Matt. 21). Palm Sunday calibrates our expectations for Holy Week to climax in Jesus' ultimate victory.

How do we celebrate it? Palm Sunday is a complete worship service, which includes these customs:

- *Palm branches.* Each worshiper is given a palm branch to wave during the processional and worship. You can purchase palm branches from a local flower shop, or use wave-ready branches from available trees or shrubs.
- *Processional.* The service can begin in a location other than your sanctuary or worship space, preferably outside. The congregation gathers, receives their palm branches, and after a welcome and call to worship, the pastor and musicians lead everyone to process into the sanctuary with songs of adoration to the King (such as "All Glory, Laud and Honor" or "Ride On! Ride On in Majesty!").
- *Passion Reading.* The passion of Jesus Christ is the "ruling narrative" of the week beginning on Palm Sunday. For that reason, many churches include a full—and in some cases dramatic—reading of Jesus' passion from one of the Gospels.

Maundy Thursday

Why do we celebrate it? We celebrate Maundy Thursday to learn how to love and serve Christ in our neighbor. On this night we live the memory of the Passover meal Jesus shared with His disciples, when our Lord washed His disciples' feet and instituted the Lord's Supper (Matt. 26:17–29; Luke 22:7–23; John 13:1–35). On this night, Jesus gave them a "new commandment" to love one another as He has loved them (John 13:34). The word *Maundy* derives from the Latin word *mandatum*, meaning "mandate" or "commandment."

We also celebrate Maundy Thursday to demonstrate how the Old Testament anticipates Jesus Christ. The symbolism of this night is beautifully layered, hearkening back to the original Passover Meal on the night before the Lord delivered His people from Egypt (Ex. 12:1–28). On Maundy Thursday, we proclaim Jesus' role as the ultimate Passover Lamb, the ultimate Suffering Servant, and the ultimate deliverer of God's people.

How do we celebrate it? The essence of the Maundy Thursday tradition is to gather with God's people to pray and feast in memory of Jesus. Your small groups could do this by hosting people in their homes. Maybe that is where you should start if you have not held a Maundy Thursday service before. I highly recommend that you eventually celebrate Maundy Thursday by gathering the whole church in a service that includes foot washing and communion.

But foot washing is super awkward to me. Yes it is, friend. Foot washing has always been awkward. It certainly was for Peter (John 13:6–7). But it is also a powerful process to learn humble love, whether we are the one washing or the one being washed. However, foot washing should never be mandatory. And I recommend only washing the feet of a family member or someone of the same gender. Do all you can to prevent this process from becoming sexualized or stimulating for certain individuals.

Foot washing logistics. One option is to use hot cloths. The advantage of this approach is the relative ease in planning and cleaning after the service. Essentially, you are providing small bins of rolled up washcloths that have been moderately doused in hot water—thus, no extra water sloshing around. Place these bins throughout the worship space along with empty bins. Worshipers can wash each other's feet by using a clean, wet cloth. When they are finished, they can place the used cloths in the empty bins. Ushers should be on call to manage the process.

Another option is to use water and towels. This is a messier process that nevertheless feels more authentic. Set up the foot-washing stations with clean towels and bins that are filled partially with warm water and wash cloths. Worshipers place their feet in the bins one at time as the person washing their feet uses a wash cloth to clean and a towel to dry. You will need a team of ushers to switch out the murky water bins with clean ones.

What is the order of service? Here's a basic outline for the service:

- Call to worship that matches the tone of the service
- Scripture readings[2]
- Sermon
- Pastoral orientation to foot washing: explain why you are observing this tradition and how it will work practically.
- Foot washing
- Worship: I recommend songs that reflect Christ's sacrificial love and that call us to Christian community (foot washing and worship are happening simultaneously).
- Communion: this is a prime opportunity to teach your congregation about the meaning of the meal that Jesus gave us.

- Make the worship space bare for Good Friday: in the Anglican tradition, we strip and wash the altar/table, remove all the banners, and shroud the cross in black cloth—symbolism that helps us live the memory of Jesus' final hours before His death.
- People are encouraged either to stay and pray or be dismissed in silence. Traditionally, no benediction is given. Why? Maundy Thursday, Good Friday, and Easter are considered to be one, seamless event, like Jesus' death and resurrection. Even though most of us go home in between the services, we are still keeping watch with Jesus.

Stations of the Cross

Why do we celebrate it? As I mentioned in chapter 14, your church can help people meditate on Jesus' journey to and through the cross with this service. As with Lent, Stations of the Cross may be celebrated by the Roman Catholic Church but is in fact a mere Christian service meant to edify all churches that proclaim the gospel. There is freedom for you to discern when and how to recognize Stations of the Cross, whether it is a formal prayer service, an open-house art gallery for the community, or a combination thereof.

What are the biblical stations?

- Jesus is in the garden of Gethsemane (Matt. 26:36–41).
- Jesus, betrayed by Judas, is arrested (Mark 14:43–46).
- Jesus is condemned by the Sanhedrin (Luke 22:66–71).
- Jesus is denied by Peter (Matt. 26:69–75).

- Jesus is judged by Pilate (Mark 15:1–5, 15).
- Jesus is scourged and crowned with thorns (John 19:1–3).
- Jesus bears the cross (John 19:6, 15–17).
- Jesus is helped by Simon the Cyrenian to carry the cross (Mark 15:21).
- Jesus meets the women of Jerusalem (Luke 23:27–31).
- Jesus is crucified (Luke 23:33–34).
- Jesus promises His kingdom to the repentant thief (Luke 23:39–43).
- Jesus speaks to His mother and the disciple (John 19:25–27).
- Jesus dies on the cross (Luke 23:44–46).
- Jesus is placed in the tomb (Matt. 27:57–60).

How do you build the stations? You can either install fourteen crosses or fourteen works of art that depict each scene. I recommend printing a guide with the Scriptures and prayers that guides people at each station. You could also post the prayers, Scripture readings, and reflections at each station.

What are we supposed to do at each station? Whether you are walking to the stations with others or alone, I recommend:

- Reading the Scripture
- Reflecting in silence on Jesus' journey to the cross, remembering that it was a journey of love for you and for the life of the world
- Asking Jesus to give you His power to bear your own cross in love for Him and others
- This can be done liturgically, silently, in song, extemporaneously, or all in combination of these

Good Friday

Why do we celebrate it? The Good Friday service is a reverent yet joyful commemoration of Jesus' death on the cross. We come ready to adore the Lamb of God who has taken away the sin of the world—once and for all. As we hear the gospel and meditate on God's love poured out for us, individually and corporately, we are freed to confess our weaknesses and sin. We do not come to Good Friday to feel sorry for Jesus. We come with gratitude and humility for the great exchange of our sin for His cleansing and righteousness.

How do we celebrate it? You may already conduct a Good Friday service. If you decide to make changes to it after reading this book, I recommend doing so incrementally and only after explaining the purpose of the adjustments to your people. Or you might be a church planter who is starting a Good Friday service for your congregation from scratch. In any case, here are elements that make Good Friday meaningful:

- Extolling Christ as our Suffering Servant (Isa. 52:13–53:12), our Great High Priest and Mediator (Heb. 10:1–25), and the Lamb of God (Gen. 22:1–18; John 18:1–19:37)
- A bare worship space: less is more on Good Friday
- A large wooden cross
- Processing with the cross: in our tradition, we carry the cross through the sanctuary during the worship service, which helps people connect with the personal nature of Jesus' sacrifice for us
- Praying at the cross: I recommend laying the cross on

the floor of the worship space and allowing people to pray at the cross.

- Prayer ministers: recruit and train ministers (lay or ordained) who can shepherd the people of God through this service; some people may be ready to confess Jesus as Lord for the first time, some will be ready to confess their sins, and others may be set free from some kind of spiritual oppression, so be ready with your best intercessors and counselors to walk them through what they need

What is the order of service?

- Begin service in silence
- Call to worship and opening prayer
- Scripture readings,[3] including the Passion Narrative (same as Palm Sunday: John 18:1–19:37)
- Sermon
- Hymn or song of response
- Prayers for the church and the world (we call this the "solemn collects")
- Procession of the cross
- Praying at the cross, during which songs or anthems are sung: this is ministry time that could potentially continue even after everyone is formally dismissed
- Concluding prayer: direct people to leave in silence; as with Maundy Thursday it is customary not to give a benediction until after the Easter celebration

Easter Vigil

What is Easter Vigil? Easter Vigil, held on the evening before Easter Sunday, is another mere Christian tradition with a rich, long history. References to this sort of service are found as early as the second century. The Easter Vigil as it is practiced today is a highly involved service. It takes industrial strength, detailed organization, and focused leadership to pull off. Before you attempt to fit it into your Holy Week lineup, remember that you already have a week packed with services. Plus, Easter Sunday is the next day, and that's when you will welcome unchurched visitors. If you have to choose between a cool service and having energy to love the unchurched, please choose the unchurched! Even if you elect not to put on a vigil, I hope you consider ways in which you can incorporate elements of the Easter Vigil into your Easter Sunday celebration. That said, I will use "Easter" and "Easter Vigil" interchangeably in the following paragraphs.

Why do we celebrate it? The Easter Vigil is our time to exult in the reality of Jesus' resurrection from the dead. We gather as God's renewed people to celebrate Jesus' victory for us over evil, sin, and death. We honor His role in inaugurating new creation, reconciling us to God and uniting heaven and earth. As I discussed in chapter 6, we come to the Easter Vigil, and Easter Sunday, to learn to love the future with recaptured imaginations, renewed commitments, and restored souls.

How do we celebrate it? The Easter Vigil has four major sections:

1. The Service of Light, or "Exsultet," which represents our pilgrimage from the darkness of Good Friday to the light of Jesus' life on Easter.

2. The Liturgy of the Word, which tells the grand story of salvation and invites our response of praise.

3. Baptisms, which include the renewal of baptismal vows on the part of the congregation.

4. The Eucharist—also known as Communion or the Lord's Supper—which begins with a declaration that Christ is risen and culminates with a joyful feast.

Unique elements of the Easter Vigil to consider for your Easter service. Begin the service in darkness, and process with a large candle that can light all the congregational candles. This helps connect the dots between Good Friday and Easter. Next, commission people in your church to memorize and dramatically recite the Vigil readings, which depict salvation history.[4] After each reading, lead the congregation in a response of praise. The readings include:

- The story of creation (Gen. 1:1–2:2)
- The flood (Gen. 7:1–5, 11–18; 8:6–18; 9:8–13)
- Abraham's sacrifice of Isaac (Gen. 22:1–18)
- Israel's deliverance at the Red Sea (Ex. 14:10–15:1)
- Salvation offered freely to all (Isa. 55)
- A new heart and a new spirit (Ezek. 36:22–28)
- The valley of dry bones (Ezek. 37:1–14)
- The gathering of God's people (Zeph. 3:12–20)
- The resurrection of Jesus (Matt. 28:1–10; Mark 16:1–8; Luke 24:1–12; John 20:1–18)[5]

After reading the resurrection account(s), a full-throated acclamation of "Alleluia! Christ is risen!" is given from the worship leader or pastor, followed by an equally loud response from the congregation of "The Lord is risen, alleluia!" You can follow this with some "holy noise" of celebration and songs of praise. You can encourage people in advance to bring their bells for this moment. Let the children dance in the aisles, and maybe let yourself join them. Lent is over! (I have included several of the liturgies we use for these services at aarondamiani.com/resources.)

If you would like more instruction, history, and ideas for these and other special services for Lent and Holy Week, see the following list of recommended resources. I do not endorse everything included in these books but find them generally helpful in planning services and understanding their history.

Recommended Resources

The Book of Common Prayer. New York: Oxford University Press, 1979.

The Worship Sourcebook, second edition. Grand Rapids: Faith Alive Christian Resources, 2013.

Leonel Mitchell, *Lent, Holy Week, Easter and the Great Fifty Days: A Ceremonial Guide.* Cambridge: Cowley Publications, 1996.

Lutheran Service Book. St. Louis: Concordia, 2006.

Mark Galli, *Beyond Smells & Bells: The Wonder and Power of Christian Liturgy.* Brewster: Paraclete Press, 2008.

The Book of Occasional Services. New York: Church Publishing, 2000.

Notes

Chapter 1: Into the Wilderness

1. Matt Jensen, *The Gravity of Sin: Augustine, Luther and Barth on "homo incurvatus in se"* (Oxford: Bloomsbury Publishing, 2006), 7.

2. The forty days of Lent begin on Ash Wednesday and end on the Saturday before Easter. Sundays in Lent do not count toward the forty days, as every Sunday belongs to the "New Creation" and is therefore a "feast" day. I will discuss this further in chapter 2.

3. Dallas Willard, *The Divine Conspiracy* (San Francisco: Harper & Row, 1998), 356.

Chapter 2: A (Mercifully Short) History of Lent

1. Stewart Ruch, "Fasting as Focus" (sermon, Church of the Resurrection, Wheaton, IL, August 29, 2010).

2. Andrew McGowen, *Ancient Christian Worship* (Grand Rapids: Baker Academic, 2014), 240–41.

3. Paul Bradshaw and Maxwell Johnson, *The Origins of Feasts, Fasts and Seasons in Early Christianity* (Collegeville, MN: Liturgical Press, 2011), 111–13.

4. Hippolytus, *The Apostolic Tradition*, 17, specifies a three-year period, although the catechumenate could be as short as two years or as long as four years. See also William Harmless, *Augustine and the Catechumenate*, rev. ed. (Collegeville, MN: Liturgical Press, 2014), 3–34.

5. Didache 6, http://www.thedidache.com; Justin, *Apology*, 61, Archive.org, https://archive.org/details/firstapologyofju00just.

6. Eusebius, *Church History*, trans. by K. Lake, Loeb Classical Library (Cambridge, MA: Harvard University Press, 1926), 5.24.

7. Bradshaw and Johnson, *The Origins of Feasts,* 99–100.

8. Ibid., 99, 91.

9. Canon 5, "The Canons of the Council of Nicea," Christian History for Everyman (website), http://www.christian-history.org/council-of-nicea-canons.html.

10. Bradshaw and Johnson, *The Origins of Feasts*, 109.

11. Herbert Lockyer, *The Lenten Sourcebook* (Grand Rapids: Zondervan, 1968), 14–15.

Chapter 3: Repeating History—the Right Way

1. For a fuller picture of the origins and excesses of Christian asceticism and its offshoots, see "The Development of Fasting from Monasticism through the Reformation to the Modern Era" in Kent Berghuis, *Christian Fasting: A Theological Approach* (Richardson, TX: Biblical Studies Press, 2007), 119–50; "History and Meaning of the Disciplines" in Dallas Willard, *The Spirit of the Disciplines* (San Francisco: Harper & Row, 1988), 130–55.

Chapter 4: Receiving the Humility of Christ

1. "The Message: You Are Beautiful," http://you-are-beautiful.com/pages/the-message.

2. I am indebted to Tim Keller's insights on identity formation that he shared in his November 11, 2015, address at Wheaton College titled "Our Identity: The Christian Alternative to Late Modernity's Story," as well as to Charles Taylor's exploration of "The Age of Authenticity" in *A Secular Age* (Cambridge, MA: Belknap Press of Harvard University Press, 2007), 459ff.

3. Many evangelical churches like my own add the phrase, "Repent and believe the gospel" or "but for the grace of Christ."

4. Jesus Himself commended the use of ashes for the purpose of repentance (Matt. 11:21). The nation of Israel used ashes in their lament before God (Est. 4:3), Jonah commended ashes to the repenting Ninevites (Jonah 3), and Job repented before the Lord in ashes (Job 42:6).

5. *The Book of Common Prayer* (New York: Oxford University Press, 1979), 265.

6. Bill Gaultiere, *Your Best Life in Jesus' Easy Yoke* (self-published, 2016), Kindle locations 2067–69.

7. Jeanne Marie Guyon, *Letters of Jeanne Guyon* (New Kensington, PA: Whitaker House, 2013), 8.

8. Alexander Schmemann, *Great Lent: Journey to Pascha* (Crestwood, NY: St. Vladimir's Seminary Press, 2001), 19.

Chapter 5: Confessing Our Secrets

1. Dietrich Bonhoeffer, *Life Together* (New York: Harper & Row, 1954), 112.

2. Two books I recommend on the subject are James K. A. Smith, *You Are What You Love: The Spiritual Power of Habit* (Grand Rapids: Brazos Press, 2016) and Mark Galli, *Beyond Smells and Bells: The Wonder and Power of Christian Liturgy* (Brewster, MA: Paraclete Press, 2008).

3. *The Book of Common Prayer* (BCP) (New York: Oxford University Press, 1979), 264. For the Scriptures behind this prayer, see Psalms 32, 51, and 1 John 1:9.

4. Ibid., 267–68.

5. Aleksandr Isaevich Solzhenitsyn, *The Gulag Archipelago 1918–1956: An Experiment in Literary Investigation* (New York: Harper & Row, 1973), 75.

6. BCP, 309. This prayer is adapted to modern language.

7. I should note that when we confess liturgically, people do not name their specific sins aloud. That would not be possible or helpful pastorally.

8. BCP, 447.

9. Tim Keller and Kathy Keller, *The Meaning of Marriage: Facing the Complexities of Commitment with the Wisdom of God* (New York: Dutton, 2011), 48.

10. BCP, 280.

11. BCP, 281.

Chapter 6: Learning to Love the Future

1. A prayer from the Easter Vigil liturgy, *The Book of Common Prayer* (New York: Oxford University Press, 1979), 290.

2. Robin M. Jensen, *Baptismal Imagery in Early Christianity: Ritual, Visual and Theological Dimensions* (Grand Rapids: Baker Academic, 2012), 170–72.

3. William Harmless, *Augustine and the Catechumenate*, rev. ed. (Crestwood, NY: St. Vladimir's Seminary Press, 2014), 309–10.

4. Ibid., 303.

5. Bryan M. Litfin, *Early Christian Martyr Stories* (Grand Rapids: Baker Academic, 2014), 94.

6. Ibid., 94–105.

7. See the "World Watch List" for Christian persecution put out every year by Open Doors, https://www.opendoorsusa.org/christian-persecution/world-watch-list/.

8. The Islamic State's beheading of twenty-one Coptic Christians on the beach of Tripoli, Libya, in 2015 has been viewed online millions of times worldwide.

9. This phrase is original to St. Cyprian of Carthage. See Bishop Kallistos Ware, *The Inner Kingdom* (Crestwood: NY: St. Vladimir's Seminary Press, 2000), 121–22.

10. This phrase describes Augustine's pastoral vision for his congregation, who struggled to leave behind the trappings and habits of paganism. Taken from Peter Brown, *Augustine of Hippo: A Biography*, rev. ed. (Berkeley, CA: University of California Press, 1999), 314.

Chapter 7: Answering Common Objections

1. Mike Fabarez, "Lent and Why I Don't," Pastor Mike Fabarez (blog), February 18, 2015, http://www.pastormike.com/lent-and-why-i-dont.

2. I. Howard Marshall, *The Pastoral Epistles* (Edinburgh: T&T Clark, 1999), 532–33.

3. Athanasius, *On the Incarnation* (Empire Books, 2013), 22.

4. Dallas Willard, *The Great Omission: Reclaiming Jesus' Essential Teachings on Discipleship* (New York: HarperCollins Publishers, 2006), 61.

5. Carl Trueman, "Ash Wednesday: Picking and Choosing Our Piety," Reformation 21 (website), February 2015, http://www.reformation21.org/articles/ash-wednesday.php.

6. William Harmless, *Augustine and the Catechumenate* (Collegeville, MN: Liturgical Press, 1996), 307.

7. This phrase is original to Abraham Heschel, *The Sabbath*, rev.ed. (New York: Farrar Straus Giroux, 1997), 8.

Chapter 8: The Mountain of Fasting

1. Scot McKnight argues that this type of fasting should be called "abstinence" to eliminate confusion with the classic discipline of fasting. See *Fasting: The Ancient Practices* (Nashville: Thomas Nelson, 2009), 20–22.

2. Rev. George Mastrantonis, "Fasting from Iniquities and Foods," Greek Orthodox Archdiocese of America (website), http://www.goarch.org/ourfaith/ourfaith8125.

3. This question originated from an Ash Wednesday sermon by Fr. Kevin Miller, "What's Your 'Gotta Have'?" preached February 21, 2007, at Church of the Resurrection (Wheaton, IL).

4. McKnight, *Fasting*, 20.

5. Alexander Schmemann, *Great Lent: Journey to Pascha* (Crestwood, NY: St. Vladimir's Seminary Press, 2001), 98.

6. Ibid., 99.

Chapter 9: The Valley of Prayer

1. Leah Libresco, "The Sun is Always Shining in Modern Christian Pop," FiveThirtyEight (website), June 2, 2016, http://fivethirtyeight.com/features/the-sun-is-always-shining-in-modern-christian-pop/.

2. Debbie Downer is a recurring character from *Saturday Night Live* who ruins otherwise happy group interactions by connecting every comment to a depressing stat or idea.

3. Walter Brueggemann, *Praying the Psalms: Engaging Scripture and the Life of the Spirit, Second Edition* (Eugene, OR: Wipf & Stock, 2007), 14 (emphasis mine).

4. Meredith Schultz, "The Troughs," Art House America (blog), accessed July 8, 2016, http://www.arthouseamerica.com/blog/the-troughs.html.

5. This last phrase is inspired by David Rosebery's article on preaching during Easter, called "Ten Ways to Preach the Easter Sermon" at Anglican Pastor, March 23, 2016, http://anglicanpastor.com/ten-easter-sermon-ideas/.

6. Paul Miller, *A Praying Life* (Colorado Springs: NavPress, 2009), 37.

7. Eugene Peterson, *The Contemplative Pastor* (Dallas: Word Publishing, 1989), 97–100.

Chapter 10: The Adventure of Almsgiving

1. John Oswalt, *The Book of Isaiah 40–66*, New International Commentary on the Old Testament, (Grand Rapids: Eerdman's, 1998), 507.

2. For an excellent resource on this subject, see Steve Corbett and Brian Fikkert, *When Helping Hurts: How to Alleviate Poverty Without Hurting the Poor* (Chicago: Moody, 2012).

3. John Ortberg, Laurie Pederson, and Judson Poling, *Giving: Unlocking the Heart of Good Stewardship* (Grand Rapids: Zondervan, 2000), 96.

4. Matt Woodley, *The Gospel of Matthew: God With Us* (Downers Grove, IL: InterVarsity Press, 2011), 181.

5. Ibid.

Chapter 11: The Cup of Confession

1. Timothy Keller and Kathy Keller, *The Meaning of Marriage* (New York: Penguin Group, 2011), 48.

2. David Powlison, *Speaking the Truth in Love* (Phillipsburg, NJ: P&R Publishing, 2003), 132–40.

3. Richard Foster, *Celebration of Discipline*, 3rd ed. (San Francisco: Harper & Row, 1998), 153.

4. *The Book of Common Prayer* (BCP) (New York: Oxford University Press, 1979), 448.

5. Ibid., 447.

6. For state-specific laws, see https://www.childwelfare.gov/pubPDFs/clergymandated.pdf or consult with a legal counselor.

Chapter 12: Tying It All Together

1. The following is modeled after Dallas Willard's "Vision, Intention, Means" process of discipleship, which can be found in his book *Renovation of the Heart: Putting on the Character of Christ* (Colorado Springs: NavPress, 2012). For me, the most helpful distillation of Willard's teaching on this process is Bill Gaultiere's book *Your Best Life in Jesus' Easy Yoke* (self-published, 2016). I recommend this "Vision, Intention, Means" process because I have found it to be a realistic way to train for Christlikeness (rather than just *trying really hard*, which doesn't work). Take note that this is a *path*, not a formula or a machine. There's nothing fast or automatic about this process—just a lifelong journey of transformation.

2. There are exceptions, of course, depending on life circumstances, which we covered in chapters 8 and 9.

3. N. T. Wright, *After You Believe* (New York: HarperOne, 2012), 35.

Chapter 13: Leading Children through Lent

1. I was particularly encouraged by Tim Challies's exhortation to lower expectations and simply read the Bible and pray with my family. See "How We Do Family Devotions," Challies.com (website), July 13, 2015, http://www.challies.com/christian-living/how-we-do-family-devotions.

2. These questions are used with permission. They are taken from *To Be a Christian: An Anglican Catechism*, the catechism written by Anglican theologian J. I. Packer and the Catechesis Task Force of the Anglican Church in North America (Ambridge, PA: Anglican House Publishers, 2014). *To Be a Christian* is available as a free download at aarondamiani.com/resources.

3. This idea comes from Lacy Fin Borgo and Benn Barczi, *Good Dirt: Lent and Eastertide for Families* (self-published, 2014), 20.

4. I am grateful for my friend Tim Brown, pastor of Grace Covenant Church in Exton, Pennsylvania, for sharing his ideas with me, including the Bitter Cup, the Good Friday Cross, and Soup Night.

5. Noel Piper and John Piper, *Treasuring God in Our Traditions* (Wheaton, IL: Crossway, 2007), 95–97.

Appendix: Special Services in Lent

1. The readings for Ash Wednesday can include: Joel 2:1–17; Isaiah 58:1–12; Psalm 103; 2 Corinthians 5:20–6:10; Matthew 6:1–21.

2. Recommended Scripture readings for Maundy Thursday include: Exodus 12; Psalm 78; 1 Corinthians 11:23–32; John 13:1–15; Luke 22:14–30.

3. Recommended selections for Good Friday include: Isaiah 52:13–53:12; Genesis 22:1–18; Psalms 22, 40, 69; John 18:1–19:37; Hebrews 10:1–25.

4. For ideas on performing memorized Scripture, go to http://www.mercuryblog.org, where Tyler Thompson shares our experience of doing this at Immanuel Anglican.

5. Technically, the reading of the Gospel comes later in the Vigil service.

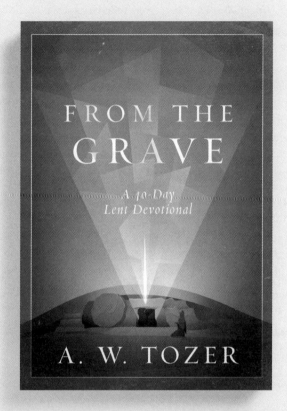

Lent is a time for recalling our death to sin and life to God. *From the Grave* aids in that by combining A. W. Tozer's best reflections on faith, suffering, and spiritual progress. Each daily reading is paired with Scripture to guide hearts in the way of the cross, the "pain-wracked path" to life.